# THE
# REFERENCE
# SHELF

# THE
# MILITARY
# DRAFT

edited by JASON BERGER

**THE REFERENCE SHELF**
Volume 53 Number 4

THE H. W. WILSON COMPANY

New York    1981

# THE REFERENCE SHELF

The books in this series contain reprints of articles, excerpts from books, and addresses on current issues and social trends in the United States and other countries. There are six separately bound numbers in each volume, all of which are generally published in the same calendar year. One number is a collection of recent speeches; each of the others is devoted to a single subject and gives background information and discussion from various points of view, concluding with a comprehensive bibliography. Books in the series may be purchased individually or on subscription.

## Library of Congress Cataloging in Publication Data

Main entry under title:

The Military draft.

(The Reference shelf; v. 53, no. 4)
Bibliography: p.
1. Military service, Compulsory—United States—
Addresses, essays, lectures. 2. Military service,
Voluntary—United States—Addresses, essays, lectures.
I. Berger, Jason. II. Series.
UB343.M49          355.2′2363′0973          81-10483
ISBN 0-8242-0656-8          AACR2

PRINTED IN THE UNITED STATES OF AMERICA

# CONTENTS

# PREFACE

Memories of antidraft protests and draft card burnings are vivid for many Americans. In the late 1960s and early 1970s, the public witnessed on television and in person marches and rallies in major cities and college towns protesting the drafting of young men for the war in Vietnam. Frequently, these peaceful demonstrations became violent. Public turmoil often turned inward and more personal when American families were forced to experience the traumatic consequences of seeing loved ones flee the U.S. to evade the draft.

In 1972 President Nixon and Congress replaced the draft with an All-Volunteer Army. Young Americans were encouraged through a combination of sophisticated recruitment techniques and financial inducements to enlist. It seemed that one of the most divisive issues of the late 1960s had been laid to rest. But eight years later President Carter in his 1980 State of the Union Address asked Congress for the budgetary authorization to begin registration for a possible draft. Citing the invasion of Afghanistan by the Soviets, the President said: "Registration for the draft is needed to increase our preparedness and is a further demonstration of our resolve as a nation."

Congress approved Carter's request and registration of nineteen-year-old men began. Although most Americans seemed to support it, college students and veteran antiwar activists protested the registration plan. The American Civil Liberties Union decided to challenge the plan in court because it excluded women, thus discriminating against men. In late July 1980 a three-judge Federal panel in Philadelphia agreed with the ACLU brief and declared the law unconstitutional. However, Justice William Brennan issued a stay overturning this decision, permitting registration to continue until the Supreme Court could rule on the case.

In a 6–3 decision handed down June 25, 1981, the Court

upheld the constitutionality of the male-only draft registration legislated by Congress. The majority opinion stated that "The case [Rostker v. Goldberg] arises in the context of Congress' authority over national defense and military affairs . . ." and ruled that Congress was within its constitutional rights in excluding women.

Although the Reagan administration has so far allowed the registration program to go on, the President, who opposed it during his campaign, has not yet taken action on the matter. For most Americans the issue is not registration so much as the fear that registration would ultimately lead to conscription. Coalitions of diverse groups are currently active both in supporting and in opposing any future draft. Their debate raises many questions that this book examines.

One important point that needs to be considered is why President Carter suddenly proposed registration. Was it, as he contended, an effort to demonstrate American power in the wake of the Soviet invasion of Afghanistan or was this merely a pretext because of doubts about the effectiveness of the volunteer army?

Section I is an analysis of the present All-Volunteer Army detailing both its strengths and weaknesses as seen by a variety of observers. Section II gives pro and con arguments by two leading U.S. senators on the need for draft registration; looks at opposing reactions to registration by two draft-age youths; and then details how the new registration rules work. Section III outlines the case in favor of a military draft while Section IV presents the antidraft position. Section V focuses on the women's issue in light of President Carter's original proposal to include women in any draft registration and the Supreme Court case on the constitutionality of the law that excludes them.

The editor thanks the authors and publishers who granted permission to reprint selections in this volume.

JASON BERGER

July 1981

# I. THE ALL-VOLUNTEER ARMY

## EDITOR'S INTRODUCTION

On September 12, 1979, the House of Representatives defeated by a vote of 252 to 163 a defense appropriation bill authorizing the commencement of standby draft registration for eighteen-year-old males in 1981. Although the proregistration, prodraft forces were decisively defeated, the fact they were able to force a full house vote on the issue reveals that many in the House questioned the efficacy of the All-Volunteer Force (AVF) and believed that reinstituting the draft was the only way to strengthen American defenses. Other observers also felt that the All-Volunteer Army had serious deficiencies and that the reserves were an inadequate backup in the event of a national emergency. Even though they failed to obtain passage of the registration bill, the prodraft forces did succeed in subjecting the concept of a volunteer army to a thorough public scrutiny.

Critics of the AVF contend that it draws most of its manpower from the poorest and least educated segments of the population. Minorities now make up over 40% of the volunteer army, while only 54% of the enlistees are high school graduates. According to Senator John Stennis: "We are not going to be able to get sufficient numbers of qualified people through the volunteer system." Few middle-class youth volunteer to join the army.

Defenders of the AVF claim the racial imbalance is immaterial and cite Drew Middleton, military affairs specialist of the *New York Times,* who reported that the volunteers are regarded "as the most effective peacetime force of this century" by their commanders and officers. President Reagan also favors a volunteer army and reportedly plans higher pay to spur recruitment as well as bonus increases for those enlistees with the most needed skills.

In the first article, Christopher A. Kojm, senior editor of the Foreign Policy Association, gives a concise summation of the state of the All-Volunteer Force. "Personnel problems fall into two categories: *recruitment* of new personnel and the *retention* of experienced personnel . . . especially people with skills which are in strong demand in the private sector, such as electronics specialists."

"Uncle Sam does want you—if you're white, bright, and ready to fight," claims Joseph Kelley writing in *The Progressive.* "The Army now relies less on the combat-ready soldier and more on technicians and specialists skilled in handling new management systems and technology."

Harry A. Marmion, author of *The Case Against a Volunteer Army* (Times Books, 1971), explains in the next article excerpted from *Commonweal* some of the reasons why he thinks the volunteer army has failed. These include first-term attrition, a declining recruitment pool, cost, and shortfalls in meeting enlistment goals. "Without doubt the volunteer system exacerbates all our national weaknesses. It is inevitably designed to make its primary appeal to the poor, minorities and the dispossessed, to whom the armed services act as an employer of last resort."

However, Bertram Gross writing in *The Nation,* responded vehemently to this claim. "The contention that the present Army volunteers are not good enough is, in part, a dangerous exercise in thinly veiled racism." He also finds it curious that "when the quality of the All-Volunteer Army is discussed, no reference is made to the quality of military leadership. It is as though the auto workers, rather than the management, were to be blamed for the economic failures of the Chrysler Corporation."

A leading military sociologist, Charles C. Moskos, Jr., concludes that in the All-Volunteer Army "the grievous flaw has been a redefinition of military service in terms of the economic marketplace and the cash-work nexus . . . The standard that military participation ought to be a citizen duty has been blurred." Writing in *Society*, he proposes a national program of citizen service by all young Americans encompassing both civilian and military options coupled with post-service educational benefits.

"Pro-draft forces are opening a Pandora's box again that had best remain closed," writes Murray Polner in *Commonweal* and goes on to refute each criticism made of the Volunteer Army. In a study ordered by the Armed Services Committee and issued under Defense Department auspices, he quotes two Pentagon military personnel specialists who dismiss "criticisms of the Volunteer Army as merely subjective [translation: political]: 'A return to the draft is no panacea for the problems of today's military.'"

The view from overseas is reflected in the next article from the London *Economist* which thinks that the quality of the AVF, the largest fighting force within NATO, has declined sharply. "The American army has become volunteer without becoming professional, a body apart, without being either elite or proud . . . Beneath a hard surface, the core is soft and spongy."

---

## MILITARY READINESS, MANPOWER AND THE DRAFT[1]

---

The humiliating failure of the military rescue mission to free the American hostages in Teheran raised sharp questions about the competence and readiness of U.S. forces.

General Edward C. Meyer, Army Chief of Staff, described his forces in the continental United States as a "hollow army," with shortages in personnel, training, weapons and equipment. A confidential Army report rated six of ten combat divisions in the United States as "not combat-ready," and three of the remaining four as combat-ready with major defi-

[1] Excerpt from *The ABC's of Defense: America's Military in the 1980s*, by Christopher A. Kojm, senior editor, and the editors of Foreign Policy Association. Headline Series 254, Ap. '81. p 55–63. Copyright 1981 Foreign Policy Association, Inc.

ciencies. The Navy has its own readiness problems: only six of thirteen U.S. aircraft carriers were rated as combat-ready in 1980, and five of the six were "marginally" ready. Only 50 percent of the Air Force's fighter planes are rated mission-capable. How disturbing is the reality behind these statements? As military analyst Edward N. Luttwak points out, it is wasteful to keep forces 100 percent ready all the time. But what levels of readiness are adequate? Have we met them?

### The 'Beans and Bullets' Side of Readiness

Funding for military readiness largely falls under the budget category of "Operations and Maintenance" (O&M). This includes funding for manpower training, repairs and spare parts, the unglamorous "beans and bullets" category that keeps the military's personnel and hardware functioning. All the services argue that they need sharp increases in O&M funding.

The *Army* in Europe, according to Melvin Laird, has a backlog of $1 billion in needed repairs and maintenance. Moreover, there are shortages of ammunition, fuel and spare parts. The Carter budgets for fiscal year (FY) '81 and '82 provide sharp increases for these items, but deliveries will take several years. The widely heralded antitank missile is so expensive ($5,000 apiece) that most of the time soldiers train on simulators. Only the best trainees get to shoot a live missile, and only once or twice per year.

Like the Army, the *Navy* suffers from a lack of spare parts and ordnance. There is such a serious shortage of Phoenix air-to-air missiles, which cost $1 million apiece, that some Navy pilots only fire a live missile every five years. Moreover, the Navy in FY '81 will not even buy enough new aircraft to replace the planes it lost the previous year through accidents and obsolescence.

The *Air Force*, like the Navy, suffers from a lack of ordnance for its planes, according to defense analyst Lawrence J. Korb. The United States traditionally has been more proficient in pilot training than the Soviets, but because of high fuel and maintenance costs, flying hours for both Air Force and Navy pilots have been curtailed.

During the 1980 presidential campaign, the state of military readiness came under fire from the Republican party. Defense Secretary Brown, speaking on the Administration's behalf, termed readiness ratings "misleading." Brown noted that if the same readiness standards were applied to the Soviet Union, two-thirds of its divisions would be rated "not ready." As in the U.S. case, this does not mean that its forces are useless—rather, that it would take time to ready them for combat. The military rating system, Brown said, "is best understood as a peacetime planning and management tool designed to identify problem areas . . ." It says very little about how a unit will actually perform in combat.

The readiness debate continues—essentially unresolvable except in war. An equally troubling aspect of military readiness, however, involves the deep-seated problems of personnel, problems largely acknowledged by both critics and defenders of today's All-Volunteer Force.

## Personnel: Quantity and Quality

In any extended conflict, the Army will rely heavily on the reserves and the National Guard. But the Army's Individual Ready Reserve, intended to provide replacements for battlefield casualties, is some 300,000 below its authorized strength of 694,000. The National Guard as well is understaffed. While some National Guard units are highly regarded by the active Army, others lack key personnel and are poorly trained.

Within the active Army, personnel problems fall into two categories: *recruitment* of new personnel and the *retention* of experienced personnel.

The Army has had particular problems with recruitment. Only 54 percent of Army enlistees are high school graduates, compared with 76 percent of the overall 19- and 20-year-old male population. The average reading level in the Army is below the ninth-grade reading level of Army training man-

uals; 37 percent of the recruits read at the seventh-grade
level. Do low reading scores make a difference? One officer
thought not: "In those [high-technology] systems you don't
need to know what makes them work, any more than you
need to know electronics to adjust a color TV set. You just
learn to work the knobs right. I came into the Army as a private 29 years ago, and I feel that soldiers today are at least as
qualified as they were then." While the soldiers of 1980 may
be as good as those of 1950, many believe that is by no means
good enough.

### Retaining Skilled Personnel

One-third of the Army's recruits do not even complete
their first term of service. Those who do finish one term have
not yet acquired combat and technical skills. The backbone of
the Army and for that matter of all the armed services are the
noncommissioned officers (NCOs), the enlisted men who serve
more than a single four-year term. But the reenlistment rate
for two- and three-term veterans—except in the Army where
it is up slightly over the last two years—dropped in 1980. Although the services are slightly above authorized manpower
levels, they are short of experienced people, especially people
with skills which are in strong demand in the private sector,
such as electronics specialists.

Why is the military short of key personnel? One important reason is pay. When the All-Volunteer Force began in
1973, it was predicated on pay scales competitive with the civilian economy. But since then military pay scales have
lagged behind the consumer price index and behind wages in
the private sector.

For enlisted men with families who are at the bottom of
the pay scale, the problem is more serious. The volunteer
Army is increasingly an army of married soldiers, and many
NCOs in the Army stationed in the United States moonlight;
second incomes and a spouse's paycheck are needed to make
ends meet. Shipment to Europe is often viewed by NCOs as a
hardship assignment because the NCO will lose his second
job; his spouse will find it difficult to get work in Germany.

Since Congress approved a military pay increase of 11.7 percent in September 1980, the services' personnel problems have improved somewhat. A bill, sponsored by Senators Sam Nunn (D-Ga.) and John W. Warner (R-Va.), and approved over the initial opposition of the Carter Administration, also increased flight pay, sea pay, housing and travel allowances. Initial results of the pay package appear promising, but more time is needed to judge whether the impact will be sustained. Critics note that this pay package will not even compensate for the loss in income due to inflation in 1980 alone. According to Melvin Laird the choice is simple: ". . . either we pay salaries high enough to retain skilled people or we settle for a military less ready to fight in the future."

## *The Draft*

One alternative to paying more for military manpower is to make service compulsory via conscription. The military draft has only been in existence for 38 years of America's 205-year history. It has always been a politically explosive issue. Draft riots in New York City in 1863 killed 1,000. The Vietnam war led to massive resistance against the draft in the 1960s. President Nixon ended the draft in 1973 in response to antiwar political pressures; registration ended two years later. The draft, however, never died as an issue, although the political climate for its restoration remained chilly—until 1980.

In the aftermath of the twin shocks of Iran and Afghanistan, President Carter in January 1980 called for the registration of 19- and 20-year-old men and women for military service. His intention was not to reactivate the draft now, but to lessen time required if it were deemed necessary later. Perhaps more important, registration was intended as a signal to friend and foe alike of America's military resolve. When the United States chided its NATO allies for their lack of military effort, the allies would remind Washington that their systems of military conscription were intact. Congress obliged President Carter and approved draft registration for men; draft registration for women was defeated, brushed aside as a "sociological experiment" by powerful Senator Nunn.

It was open to question just what draft registration would achieve. Senator Nunn claimed that in a crisis it would cut 90 days off the time needed to get draftees to report for basic training. Selective Service Director Bernard D. Rostker, on the other hand, had told President Carter before he approved it that registration was "redundant and unnecessary." It would save only 7 days—117 versus 124—in getting draftees through military training, which was still well within the Pentagon's 180-day war plan.

Advocates of the draft hoped, and its opponents feared, that registration was a stalking horse: if registration came, could the draft be far behind?

## Arguments in Support of the Draft

The armed services face a coming crisis of manpower. Because of the declining birthrates in the 1960s, the number of young men who reach age 18 will fall from 2.1 million in 1980 to 1.7 million by 1987. To maintain current force levels, the military will need to attract 1 out of every 4.6 18-year-olds, instead of 1 out of every 5.6, as is now the case.

All four services, for the first time, fell short of their recruiting goals in 1979. In 1980 the picture improved in part because of the impact of the recession and the September pay raise. Nonetheless, an Army draft would bolster the manpower outlook for all the services, because experience has shown that for many young men enlistment in the other three services is preferable to Army induction. For the same reason the draft would also ease the personnel problems of the Army reserve.

According to draft proponents, only a draft can raise the quality of enlisted personnel. Many senior officers prefer the draft because draftees are better disciplined than recruits, and some military observers prefer it as a means of holding down personnel costs and freeing money for military hardware.

In today's All-Volunteer Force, the percentage of minorities in the Army is 41 percent; in the Marine Corps, 26 percent. Should future wars be fought by the poor and the non-white because the white middle class could avoid military service? In addition, today over 40 percent of U.S. males have served in the military. But that percentage is dropping. What are the implications for our security when both tomorrow's leadership elite and the general public have no military experience?

Even if the draft itself is not restored, shouldn't there be a broad requirement for mandatory national service? This kind of program would place equal demands on all young people, avoiding the deeply divisive question of "who shall serve?"

## The Draft: Why We Don't Need It

For many, the draft is an irrelevant issue. Economist Milton Friedman writes, "Grant [the draft] every virtue proponents attribute to it, and major personnel problems would remain. Solve those problems, and the military arguments for conscription evaporate." He believes that if the pay scales were right, the military could get suitable people in both sufficient quantity and quality. Civilian contracting of military-support jobs would also allow a greater number of today's soldiers to concentrate on essential military activities.

Former Secretary of the Army Clifford L. Alexander, Jr., is also strongly opposed to the draft. He feels that it would harm the armed forces, undermining their prestige and support as was the case during the Vietnam war. Alexander, who is black, also takes great offense at critics who say that today's All-Volunteer Army is "disproportionately" black. What difference does it make who is in the Army, as long as there is equal opportunity and a soldier does his or her job?

Another problem with the draft is that its proponents are thinking in terms of World War II—a long, conventional war that requires vast manpower. But in the nuclear era, skirmishes in the third world involving small forces are more likely (if just as dangerous). Forces will need to be highly skilled; massive armies of recruits will not fill the bill.

Personnel problems can be answered in other creative

ways. Military sociologist Charles C. Moskos, Jr., advocates a new veterans' benefit bill to guarantee a college education to those who serve a hitch in the military. Another way of making up the slack in personnel is to recruit young women. Women in the services today are better educated than their male counterparts, score higher on skills tests and present fewer disciplinary problems. Women in the military totaled only 43,000 in 1973, but numbered 150,000 in 1980 and may number 250,000 by 1985, or about 12 percent of the entire force. Should women in the future continue to be restricted by law from combat categories? Most Pentagon officials feel that the range of jobs for women should be wider.

For many, the most persuasive arguments against the draft are philosophical. Thomas Jefferson and Daniel Webster opposed conscription. Today, a broad spectrum of opinion, from President Reagan to Senator Edward M. Kennedy (D-Mass.), also believes that compulsory military service is incompatible with individual liberty.

Critics on the left maintain that if a draft had not been in place in the 1960s, an American president would have found it far more difficult to commit ground forces to the war in Vietnam. As it was, President Johnson opposed General William C. Westmoreland's February 1968 request for 206,000 more troops for Vietnam because he would have had to call up the reserves, a political cost he was unwilling to pay. "Registration," these critics on the left claim, "is the first step to the draft and the first step to war."

## BEHIND THE PUSH TO REVIVE THE DRAFT[2]

Uncle Sam does want you—if you're white, bright, and ready to fight. And that may be why he's thinking about put-

[2] Reprint of magazine article by Joseph Kelley, a New York free-lance writer. *The Progressive.* 44: 23–4. My. '80. Reprinted by permission from *The Progressive*, 408 West Gorham Street, Madison, Wisconsin 53703. Copyright © 1980, The Progressive, Inc.

ting the draft back to work: The U.S. Army is short on white men with managerial or technical know-how.

With the modern Army's need for specialized skills increasing annually, Pentagon officials are worried about plummeting enlistment standards, a rash of applications for early discharge, and a serious decline in the number of well-educated white soldiers. The recent enthusiasm for renewing the draft may have less to do with events in Iran and Afghanistan than it does with a desire to expand the pool of white enlisted men who arrive with professional or technical skills.

The personnel structure of the military today bears a close resemblance to the civilian sector in its reliance on a class of professional managers. As a 1979 study by the Brookings Institute clearly demonstrated, the Army now relies less on the combat-ready soldier and more on technicians and specialists skilled in handling new management systems and technology. "We can not get enough of the right kind of people, with the necessary skills and abilities to fit the needs," Senator John Stennis, Mississippi Democrat, has said of the present volunteer Army.

Given the educational and economic realities of American society, solving that problem through the draft can only mean pumping more white inductees—especially those with some college training—into what is already a two-tiered structure. While officers, mid-level managers, and technicians are overwhelmingly white, infantrymen and ditch diggers—plain soldiers—tend to be black.

The new Selective Service could be just that: a way to select soldiers that guarantees a supply of men for the managerial class that runs today's Army—and ensures a more comfortable racial balance. Since the old draft ended in 1972, the total number of blacks in the Army has increased by 103,000 while the number of whites has dropped by approximately 400,000. As a result, black enlistees now account for 30 percent of the army, lumped at the bottom of the military hierarchy. Black men account for only 6.1 percent of the officer corps.

The imbalance shows no signs of reversing; in fact, it is almost certain to grow in the coming years. The low birth rate of the mid-1960s will leave recruiters with only 1.8 million eligible young men by 1985, down from 2.1 million today. From that number, 400,000 new soldiers must be drawn in order to maintain the troop level at its current two million men. But recruiters must compete for the best-educated candidates with equally aggressive college admissions officers, the civilian job market, and other Government programs.

As a result, the armed services five years from now are likely to be even less representative of the general population in race and economic status. Representative Robin L. Beard, Tennessee Republican, predicted recently that almost half of the junior enlisted ranks in the Army would soon be black, as well as 65 per cent of the noncommissioned officers. "I think you're going to have problems," he warned.

The problems anticipated by Beard and other critics of the present volunteer system range from racial tension to the possibility of large-scale disobedience of orders in the event of an African war. There is no real precedent for such resistance on racial or political grounds, but the possibility has received greater public attention lately as turmoil in the Middle East and Africa arouses conflicting feelings among American blacks.

Joseph Mashariki, head of the Black Veterans for Social Justice, a community organization in Brooklyn's Bedford-Stuyvesant district, asserts that black antiwar protest has always been distinct from the white movement, and that the division will become more apparent if troops are ever sent to Africa. "There was resistance in Vietnam to white people telling black people to kill yellow people," he says. "There will be resistance now, too."

The Department of Defense does not publicly acknowledge that a growing black presence in the military is an issue at all. "We look for people to perform specific functions," says an Army spokesman. "We don't feel race enters in."

At a 1974 race relations-equal opportunity conference at the Department of the Army, the matter was discussed and then dropped after participants concluded it was "desirable" to have a "cross section," but that "there should be little concern as to whether the Army is mostly one race or another."

Nevertheless, observers who deal with the military on a regular basis say high-ranking officers privately express deep concern over race and education levels in the armed forces—and reinstitution of the draft is their way of responding to the problem. If a draft lottery were implemented without loopholes, the number of blacks entering the service would fall to one in nine, while the steady decline in white enlistments would be reversed.

"Afghanistan is just a smokescreen for bringing back the draft," says military sociologist Charles Moskos of Northwestern University. "They don't want to admit the problems they have been having with the volunteer Army."

Moskos is also concerned about the racial proportions in the military, if for different reasons. In the past, he points out, the services offered poor enlistees an opportunity to compete on equal terms against the privileged. But in an Army composed mainly of the poor and the black, this chance is lost.

Along with sociologist Morris Janowitz of the University of Chicago, Moskos has proposed a series of changes in the volunteer system which would lure whites into the services and keep them from becoming a "racial enclave." These include a program of post-service educational benefits and a requirement that all inductees have high school diplomas.

But neither a reinstated draft nor an altered volunteer system sits well with those who feel such efforts pose hazards for non-white Americans. "Any attempt to define the bases and limits of black participation in the military, even under the guise of altruism, should be suspect on the reasonable expectation that blacks would emerge as losers," argues John Butler, a sociologist at the University of Texas.

If the experience of Vietnam is any indication, a reinstated draft would not make the distribution of men within the armed forces more equitable in any case. Casualties in Southeast Asia were greatest among members of lower-income groups, both black and white. And there is simply no assuring that the new system would be more free of loopholes for the privileged than its predecessor in the Vietnam era, when most upper-income white men avoided military service altogether or found safe posts away from the combat zone.

It's fair to say the volunteer Army still has big problems. The shortage of manpower in such mid-level jobs as aviation repair specialist, electrician, and tank mechanic is acute. But it's also fair to ask just what the Army is doing about it. For many of the young blacks who now fill the ranks, the service was presented as a matchless opportunity to acquire specialized training. The continuing stratification of the Army— blacks at the bottom, whites at the top, blacks on the firing line, whites manning technical posts—suggests that the real problem has to do with unkept promises rather than with the dangers of racial imbalance.

---

## AGAINST THE ALL-VOLUNTEER FORCE: IT JUST ISN'T WORKING[3]

---

. . . *Cost.* In 1978 the General Accounting Office reported that the all-volunteer force had cost $18 billion more than the draft would have if it had remained in effect.

*Inelasticity.* Should there be a legitimate national need to increase the AVF even by as much as 15 percent, there would be recruiting shortfalls and a draft would be necessary.

*Shortfalls in meeting new goals.* Each of the services has recently been unable to meet new enlistment goals. Each service has done what it could, but now it is clear that even the Air Force with its extensive training and school opportunities did not meet its December 1978 quotas. At times the services have been forced to offer a bonus to high school graduates who would join the combat arms. Of course, the higher the unemployment rate the more apt the military is to be able to meet its goals, so that these shortfalls may be cyclical. Still, it

[3] Excerpted from magazine article by Harry A. Marmion, educator and author of *The Case Against the Volunteer Army. Commonweal.* 106:555–7. O. 12, '79. Copyright © 1979 by Commonweal. Reprinted by permission.

would be ironic and unpalatable to rely on recession as a mainstay of military manpower policy.

*First-term attrition.* During the Vietnam war when the draft was in force about 20 percent of those inducted dropped out for a variety of reasons during the first years of service. In 1977, when the last figures were made public, more than 40 percent of recruits in the all-volunteer force dropped out before completing their first term. This sharp increase was attributed to literacy problems, medical problems, lack of discipline, financial hardship and inability to perform to the standards necessary in a sophisticated military.

*Weakness of the Reserves and National Guard.* This problem area of military preparedness is least understood by the public but one of the most important reasons why the Joint Chiefs of Staff are talking about a change in the way in which military manpower needs are met. During the Korean War some reserve units that were activated were decimated in combat—causing severe political problems at home. During the Vietnam conflict, reserves were not called; this, too, caused severe political problems at home. One of the cornerstones of the all-volunteer concept was to keep the active military establishment reduced as much as possible and increase the Reserve and Guard capacity to enable activation within 60 or 90 days after a conflict begins. But this strategy cannot be accomplished for the simple reason that without a draft the alternative of service in the reserves or National Guard no longer attracts the numbers needed. Those who volunteer for the active military and leave after their first term of service are likewise not being attracted to the various back-up components. This then is the most critical problem for the Joint Chiefs. How can the military mobilize the reinforcement that might have to be rushed to Europe, for example, in the event of a military crisis? The army needs an active Reserve of 750,-000. The individual ready reserve, the hardest hit of all reserve components, has declined from 1.6 million to 360,000 men in recent years.

*Unreadiness for crisis.* Last fall a nationwide exercise took place to test the capacity of the armed forces to react to limited military crisis. The results were a disaster. The Reserves are not ready; the National Guard, like the VFW and the American Legion, is a declining social club for some in the lower middle class. There are shortages of medical personnel, especially doctors and dentists in both the active and reserve forces, and never in the history of AVF have quotas in these areas been met. Further, the selective service machinery, virtually dismantled from 1972–1976, is in "deep freeze" with fewer than one hundred employees in Washington, no state headquarters and no local draft boards. It would take almost four months to induct the first draftee and another two months to conscript 100,000. Training time would be minimal. By the time we were ready to get troops to Europe probably only the islands of Iona, Jersey and Ireland would be available to save.

*Declining recruitment pool.* The demographer's message is clear and unambiguous: the number of 18-year-olds will decline by almost 25 percent from 1975 to 1980. The military has belatedly recognized the difficulty this signifies for recruiting and the potential conflict between the military, colleges and universities and industry. Higher education had long been preparing for the downturn in the traditional student population but the military felt that in a time of high national unemployment the all-volunteer force, with higher salaries, could meet military needs.

Only now does the combination of factors just discussed bring the Joint Chiefs of Staff, Congress, parts of the general public, and even the administration to the realization that the AVF is not the answer. So the Joint Chiefs are not so subtly pressing for the restoration of the standby draft system that existed in the first years of the all-volunteer force. It would require registration and possibly even testing of draft-age youth. It could also provide for a draft into the Reserves, after a short period of training. There are those who say such changes will increase the possibility of military adventures. The days of actions based on Gulf of Tonkin resolutions are long passed, however. No one seriously can believe that any administration would embark on such a course.

Several other important factors are at work in this debate. The military opposes an overhaul of its retirement system, now costing $10 billion a year. The growing recruiting problems give the military a certain leverage with Congress, and the administration is protecting the system. The line of argumentation is clear: "If we can't recruit people now, you can imagine how tough it would be with a new, modified, less favorable retirement program." Many already in the military, especially first and second termers, would also leave if the retirement system changed.

Without doubt the volunteer system exacerbates all our national weaknesses. It is inevitably designed to make its primary appeal to the poor, minorities and the dispossessed, to whom the armed services act as an employer of last resort. This is true especially when cyclical civilian unemployment is high. Unemployment among young eligible blacks is twice the nation's average and reaches 40 percent in some urban centers. It is not surprising that 40 percent of the Army's male recruits in the fall of 1978 were black.

No problem is more worrisome than the shortage of middle class recruits. Illiteracy creates serious problems for recruiting. In Detroit one out of ten youths can pass the Navy literacy test. Three out of ten in Detroit pass the Army test; in New York City the figure is 3.5 out of ten and in Los Angeles four out of ten.

Despite the government's position on affirmative action, the military still lags in the recruitment of women. The military needs about 400,000 new recruits each year to fill its ranks. Approximately 10 percent or 40,000 of these currently are women. A significant increase in this category of recruiting would relieve some of the pressure. . . .

## THE DRIVE TO REVIVE THE DRAFT[4]

A powerful drive is now under way in Washington to register young people for future military conscription. At least one of the plans—"passive" or "faceless" registration by means of a computerized central file—is shrouded in bureaucratic secrecy and media indifference. Another, "national youth service" or "universal service," has received some strained praise but little recognition of what it really is—a militarist project decked out in pseudo-liberal finery. But in whatever guise, the drive to resurrect conscription of the young represents a new and dangerous threat both to constitutional democracy and to the safety and security of the American people. . . .

### Backdoor Draft

Within the [Carter] Administration, the Pentagon brass generally favor a draft "eventually" and registration right now. Clifford Alexander, Secretary of the Army, supports the pending legislation for active registration. Secretary of Defense Harold Brown wrote in a letter dated June 8, 1978, to Senator William S. Cohen, Republican of Maine, that instead of peacetime registration now, "the proper course of action is to enhance the standby ability of the Selective Service System, including its computer resources." This view was echoed on July 6 by James McIntyre, director of the Office of Management and Budget: "It is not necessary to impose this burden [i.e., active registration] on our nation and its youth when there are effective ways to improve the capability of the Selective Service System." Stuart Eizenstat, the President's do-

[4] Excerpted from magazine article by Bertram M. Gross, Distinguished Professor of Public Policy, Hunter College and author of *Friendly Fascism. Nation.* 229:553–65. O.20, '79. Copyright © 1979 The Nation Associates.

mestic policy adviser, has said, "The Administration opposes new legislation to reimpose peacetime registration for the draft. The President already has adequate authority to require registration if circumstances warrant."

At a "town meeting" in Bardstown, Kentucky, on July 31, the President himself confused the situation by saying, "We are now reassessing the question of whether young people should be required to register at the age of 18. We might have to have registration for the draft as a precautionary measure." At a news briefing the next day, Press Secretary Jody Powell tried to clarify matters by stating that the President "remains opposed to proposals before the Congress that would mandate registration," and talking vaguely about correcting certain deficiencies in the Selective Service System. One of the realities being hidden by this executive fan dance may now be stated clearly: Passive registration is the back door through which a revived Selective Service could ultimately enter.

Computerized registration holds great attractions for the kind of people who favor central dossiers on all Americans and a waiver of most privacy laws governing access to school and government records. Moreover, once the first registration lists are run off, it will be pointed out that conscientious objectors and others are mixed in with the eligibles. This would produce both confusion and delay on "mobilization day," it will be argued. So, to avoid these delays and also to protect the conscientious objectors themselves, they will be given the privilege of coming to or writing the Selective Service in order to clarify their status. This would be a step toward the systematic classification—with physical and mental examinations, and all the rest—of all potential inductees on the list. Finally, the Big Brother approach has apparently diluted opposition to registration. Many of the most dedicated opponents of the draft have concentrated their fire on active registration without taking faceless registration seriously. Indeed, Representative Les Aspin, Democrat from Wisconsin—a stalwart liberal opponent of the Pentagon's elephantiasis—has become a leading advocate of doing the job with computers.

## The Draft Drive's Dangerous Premises

Some advocates of registration for a draft insist that the volunteer Army, which replaced the draft in 1972, has been a failure. Others—mainly Army officers, proud of the volunteer Army—say that while it has worked well thus far, it must now be replaced or supplemented by a draft. Most agree, however, that voluntary enlistments cannot be relied upon to meet the need for soldiers during the 1980s. They offer a variety of reasons: (1) the military effectiveness of the present volunteer Army is not what it should be, (2) the armed forces, including the Reserves, are not large enough, and (3) more and better soldiers will be needed in the 1980s, and they cannot be obtained without a draft.

The contention that the present Army volunteers are not good enough is, in part, a dangerous exercise in thinly veiled racism. "The volunteer force is a disaster," proclaims Representative Robin Beard, Republican from Tennessee. Echoing the dismay of some Army brass over the fact that blacks are now 34 percent of all new recruits, Beard frankly spells out the kind of disaster he fears: "If current enlistment trends continue, 45 percent of the junior enlisted ranks in the Army by 1980 will be black and 65 percent of the noncommissioned officers." Another leader of the pro-draft forces, Senator Nunn, argues that the all-volunteer Army is "on the ragged edge of viability" and "will not work in the future." Sexism also rears its head. The number of female members of the armed forces rose from 1.9 percent in 1972 to 5.7 percent in 1977. The proposed registration program, it is thought, would help attain more "acceptable" percentages of white males. In this connection, it should be noted that the Senate and House bills and the proposed passive registration program are intended for males only.

More outspoken are the critics of the low educational level of the volunteer Army. Although this charge is true in a general sense, it is also applicable to the armed services as a whole: less than 2 percent of the total personnel have college degrees. As for the new volunteers, the proportion of high school graduates and the average I.Q. level are both higher than in the previous draft Army. True, there seems to be a shortage of doctors and skilled electronic experts. If so, this is hardly a problem to be handled by registering or drafting 18-year-olds.

The steadily rising rate of less-than-honorable discharges—15 percent of all discharges as of 1977—is also pointed to as a weakness in the present Army, and during the 1973–77 period more than 400,000 were discharged in this fashion, with serious effects on their opportunities for civilian employment. But a review of many of these cases by the A.C.L.U. suggests that the fault lies mainly with antediluvian and vindictive personnel policies. Most of the volunteers joined up to escape unemployment and to get some training not otherwise available. As the country's largest "equal opportunity" employer, the Army has helped young blacks and Hispanics to escape the agony of the devastating depression suffered in urban ghettos. Many of the new volunteers, it might be added, have found that the educational opportunities have been greatly exaggerated by recruitment officers, and their treatment in the armed forces has often been excessively rough.

Curiously, when the quality of the all-volunteer Army is discussed, no reference is made to the quality of military leadership. It is as though the auto workers, rather than the management, were to be blamed for the economic failures of the Chrysler Corporation. From the Joint Chiefs down, the aping of corporate management practice has developed the "officer as entrepreneur" and created a "personnel turbulence" in which 80 percent of the Army's people changed assignments in 1978. According to Richard Gabriel and Paul Savage (*Crisis in Command* [Hill & Wang, '78]) those command defects have been "the equivalent of a military disaster."

### Pentagon Wish List

Turning to the question of quantity, we see at present a war force of more than five million people. Two million of these are in uniform (of whom almost a quarter are abroad), another two million or so are in the ready, standby and retired Reserves, and the remaining one million are Defense Department civilians. This does not include the much larger number in war industries, outer space exploration (which always has military implications), war research, war think tanks and veterans' assistance. In "The U.S. Military Posture for FY 1980," the Joint Chiefs of Staff ask for three additional U.S. divisions to reinforce the G.I.s in West Germany. In addition, the President subsequently asked the Pentagon to build a new Rapid Deployment Force capable of moving quickly into the Middle East, Africa or Latin America. In his January 1979 Congressional report supporting the President's request for war funds, Secretary of Defense Brown called for a substantial beefing up of the Reserves. If any of these requests had been based on Carter's so-called "zero-based budgeting," one could find some facts on how *present* personnel are being utilized and just why additions are needed. In the absence of such analysis, one must suspect that the so-called "military requirements" are little more than a wish list.

Even the conservative American Enterprise Institute has challenged this wish list. In his *Manpower for Military Mobilization*, Kenneth J. Coffee, a former Pentagon and Selective Service official, suggests that "the Pentagon planners have set manpower requirements without a careful in-depth evaluation of needs—a common practice during the manpower-rich draft years." In *The Price of Defense*, the Boston Study Group calls for a 50 percent reduction in the strength of the Army Reserve on the ground that their skills are associated with "light division adventurism" in Third World countries. Martin Binkin of the Brookings Institution suggests that demands for a large Reserve are more related to political influence than to genuine security. No one really knows, though, because the secrecy fog is so thick. Thomas Alder, publisher of the *Military Law Reporter*, has filed a Freedom of Information Act request to obtain the Pentagon's classified memorandum on which the current requests are based.

At a lower level of analysis, the registration-draft proponents complain that recruitment targets have been missed for the past three consecutive quarters. But this argument (echoed in a *New York Times* editorial of September 4 [1979]) misses the major point—namely, that targets for total force strength (apart from the Reserves) are being substantially met by increased re-enlistments, possibly due to the bleak employment opportunities in the civilian job market.

What *The New York Times* seems to have ignored (but the officer corps understands full well) is that the larger the Army, the greater the opportunities for promotion. Under Selective Service, officers would be selectively better served—that is, according to rank—by more, better-trained and whiter liaison officers, media experts, systems analysts, masseurs, masseuses, file clerks, chauffeurs, waiters and bartenders. And with draftees paid lower wages than enlistees, more money might be available for equipment contracts and the *dolce vita* of swivel-chair generals, procurement colonels and their military-industrial complex buddies.

## Needs of the 1980s

But what about the 1980s? Although the Joint Chiefs of Staff boast that "the United States remains as the premier world power," they warn against growing Soviet military capabilities. Leaving our shores to become NATO's Supreme Commander, Gen. Bernard Rogers warns that in the early 1980s "we should be prepared to be tested." If the tests he refers to involve new military intervention by U.S. forces— whether in the Persian Gulf oilfields, Latin America or Africa—he is fostering the old delusion, as manifested most recently by longtime U.S. support for the Shah of Iran and Somoza in Nicaragua, that military force can solve political, economic and moral problems.

But if more soldiers *were* really needed in the 1980s, could they be secured without a draft? Of course they could. Many more people could be recruited and retained by reducing the many racist and sexist barriers still existing in both the services and the Reserves. Much more could be done to curtail boot-camp barbarism. Many jobs in the military could be filled by civilians; far too much has been made of the time-worn idea that people performing support functions (the majority of the war force) should wear uniforms. More volunteers could be attracted by a sharp raise in the emoluments of reservists and the base pay of recruits—without raising a private's base pay above what state troopers, policemen or firemen receive. Large numbers of highly trained people could be obtained by upping the retirement age. Few people seem to know that "the typical new enlisted retiree is only 39 years old," as Martin Binkin points out in his authoritative *Youth or Experience? Manning the Military* (Brookings Institution, 1979). This "youth and vigor" mystique masks the fact that in almost all military work, as Binkin writes, "experience is worth more than physical prowess," and that in any case, only 16 percent of all armed forces personnel have combat jobs (30 percent in the Marines, 29 percent in the Army, 5 percent in the Navy and 2 percent in the Air Force). If the present twenty-year minimum length of service were raised to thirty, most of the present demand for specially skilled personnel could be met through retention.

Also, quite a few American G.I.s could be moved from where they are least needed to where they are most needed. To maintain more than 208,000 American troops in West Germany is a boondoggle. Assuming there is any reality to the military establishment's fears of a Russian invasion of Western Europe, there are certainly enough Western Europeans capable of handling their own self-defense. If Nixon's Vietnamization made sense, why not more Europeanization of NATO? At most, a "tripwire" force of 30,000, like that in South Korea, might be needed. . . .

. . . Promptly in 1981, according to Duane Shank of the Committee Against Registration and the Draft, and other Washington observers, the real drive for bringing back the draft will start rolling. To prepare for it, during 1980, one must remember the words of retired Marine Col. James Donovan: "The simplest, speediest and most readily understandable means of controlling militarism is to cut military manpower strengths and to reduce defense appropriations."

## NATIONAL SERVICE AND THE
## ALL-VOLUNTEER FORCE[5]

Since January 1973 the United States has sought to accomplish what it has never attempted before—to maintain two million persons on active duty on a completely voluntary basis. Now into its seventh year, the all-volunteer force has been analyzed in a seemingly endless series of studies and reports. The commentators tend to divide into two groups: those who believe the all-volunteer force is a success, and those who see little prospect of a viable defense force short of returning to a form of compulsory military service. I place myself in neither camp.

The problems of the all-volunteer force are not found in the end of conscription, or in the declining youth cohort of the 1980s, or in the efforts of service recruiters. The grievous flaw has been a redefinition of military service in terms of the economic marketplace and the cash-work nexus. The redefining process was given powerful expression by the 1970 President's Commission on an All-Volunteer Force, better known as the Gates Commission. It is a theme that recurs in official assessments of the all-volunteer force. This redefinition has contributed to moving the American military away from an institutional format to one more and more resembling that of an occupation. The standard that military participation ought to be a citizen duty has been blurred.

My focus is on that part of the all-volunteer force which relied most directly on the draft—the enlisted ranks of the Army. It must be emphasized, however, that all of the armed services were indirect beneficiaries of the selective service system. The draft was also the major impetus for recruitment into reserve and national guard components and into ROTC programs.

[5] Reprinted from magazine article by Charles C. Moskos, Jr., professor of sociology, Northwestern University and author of *Peace Soldiers. Society.* 17:70–2. N. '79. Published by permission of Transaction, Inc. from SOCIETY, Vol. 17, No. 1. Copyright © 1979 by Transaction, Inc.

The educational levels of non-prior service (NPS) male enlistees in the all-volunteer Army are lower than either the equivalent civilian population of young men or the Army entrants of 1964, the last peacetime year before the war in Vietnam. Since the end of the draft, an average of 60 percent of male Army entrants have possessed a high school diploma. This compares with 81 percent among 19-20 year-old males in the general population, and 71 percent of draftees in 1964. The contrast between the educational levels of the all-volunteer Army and the peacetime draft Army is even more glaring when placed in the context of the overall increase of male high school graduates over the past decade and a half. There is also convincing evidence that those high school graduates who do enter the service tend to be from among the weaker students in their high schools. It is revealing to look at actual numbers as well. In 1964 over 40,000 persons with some college education entered the Army's enlisted ranks; in 1978 the figure was less than 5,000.

The rising proportion of minority entrants has generated controversy in the debate on the all-volunteer Army. In 1978 black accessions made up 35 percent of NPS males. The rise in black content reflects the large increase in the proportion of blacks eligible for military service (through higher educational levels and better aptitude scores), the appallingly high unemployment rate among black youth in the 1970s, and the appeal of an organization that has gone further than any other to attack racism. Although the number of other minorities is not as reliably tabulated, a growing proportion of Army entrants are of Hispanic background. But to take note of the minority composition of the Army must not direct attention away from the participation—or, better, lack of it—of the larger white middle-class population.

It is important to stress that the decline in educational levels of NPS male recruits is *not* correlated with the rising number of black servicemen. Since the end of the draft, the proportion of black high school graduates entering the Army has exceeded that of whites, and by quite a substantial margin. What is happening in the all-volunteer Army is that whereas the black soldier is fairly representative of the black community, white entrants of recent years are coming from the least educated sectors of the white population. In my stays with Army line units I am most impressed by what I do not often find—urban and suburban white soldiers of middle-class background. The all-volunteer Army is attracting not only a disproportionate number of minorities, but also an unrepresentative segment of white youth, who, if anything, are even more uncharacteristic of the broader population than are our minority soldiers.

No change in the all-volunteer force has received as much media attention as the growing numbers and roles of women service members. A strong argument could be made that female entrants have been the margin of success in the all-volunteer force. The crux of the issue remains the prohibition of women in the ground combat arms and aboard warships. Leaving aside the considerable legal, normative, and organizational difficulties in the assignment of women to combat roles, a removal of the ban is not a solution to all-volunteer recruitment. Enlisted women are not clamoring for a major expansion of their numbers into combat roles. The recruiting successes in attracting women almost certainly would be reversed if combat assignments were given to females. Considering the difficulties in getting men to volunteer for combat roles, it is simple-minded in the extreme to believe women would be any more willing. The services already are finding it increasingly difficult to attract high quality enlisted women as more and more females are assigned to "non-traditional tasks" in the military.

An unanticipated consequence of the all-volunteer force has been a dramatic change in the marital composition of the services. From 1964 to 1979, the proportion of marrieds at the junior enlisted levels has doubled. This sharp increase in the number of young enlisted marrieds runs directly counter to national trends toward increasingly later marriages. This has caused accompanying social and economic costs in the operation of the all-volunteer force. Military readiness suffers especially with the growing number of service couples and single parents.

The lower ranks of the peacetime Army before Vietnam

were never a mirror image of American society, but the all-volunteer Army is much less representative of the American middle class than was the pre-Vietnam Army. The real question is how high-powered commissions and well financed studies by the Defense Department come up with the opposite conclusion. To ask what kind of society excuses its privileged from serving in the ranks of its military is not to argue that the makeup of the enlisted ranks be perfectly calibrated to the social composition of the larger society. But if participation of persons coming from less advantaged backgrounds in leadership positions is properly used as a measure of democratic character, it is even more important that participation of more advantaged groups in the rank and file also be a measure of representative democracy.

The issue is more than morality, it is also one of military effectiveness. There is a clear relationship between socio-educational background and soldierly performance. High school graduates, compared with high school dropouts, are twice as likely to complete their enlistments. Other measures such as combat effectiveness, enlisted productivity, and low indiscipline rates show the same positive correlation with socio-educational background. The evidence is also clear, contrary to conventional wisdom, that better educated soldiers perform better across the board—in "low skill" as well as "high skill" jobs.

By no means does being middle class make one braver or more able; there are many outstanding soldiers in the all-volunteer Army who have modest educational attainments. But our concern must also be with the chemistry of unit cohesion which requires an optimum blend of talents and backgrounds. The distinctive quality of the enlisted experience starting with World War II was the mixing of the social classes and, starting with the Korean War, the mixing of the races. This gave less-advantaged youth an opportunity to test themselves, often successfully, against more privileged youth. This state of affairs began to diminish during the Vietnam War when the college educated avoided service; it has all but disappeared in the all-volunteer Army.

The Army is not the only service competing for qualified people. All of the services have been sorely pressed to meet recruitment goals since the end of the draft, despite an active-duty level that is some 500,000 fewer than before Vietnam. It is difficult to reconcile official Pollyannaish assessments of the all-volunteer force with the realities we are confronting.

A main presumption of the Gates Commission was that with longer-term initial enlistments—four years is currently the standard—there would be less personnel turnover than in a military system heavily dependent upon draftees and draft-motivated volunteers. This has turned out not to be the case. The all-volunteer force has been plagued by high attrition rates. More than one in three recruits fail to complete initial enlistments and instead are discharged for job inaptitude, personality disorders, or disciplinary reasons. In reality, the early discharge often masks a kind of "quitting" the military. The desertion rates in the all-volunteer era, moreover, are twice that of the pre-Vietnam period. The current desertion rates are especially troublesome because they occur on top of the unprecedentedly high attrition figures.

Underlying the attrition and desertion phenomena is a source of enlisted discontent that has no counterpart in the peacetime draft era. This is what I term post-entry disillusionment. In all-volunteer recruitment, a consistent theme—out of necessity, to be sure—has been on the self-serving aspects of military life, notably, on what the service can do for the recruit in the way of training in skills transferable to civilian jobs. The irreconcilable dilemma is that many military assignments—mostly, but not exclusively, in the ground combat arms and aboard warships—do not and cannot have transferability to civilian occupations. It is precisely in such military assignments that attrition and desertion are most likely to occur.

It is time to reassess our experience of the all-volunteer force. Present and anticipated difficulties in recruitment have led to renewed arguments to restore conscription. Yet it is indisputable that public opinion supports the all-volunteer concept. If induction is used, many will attempt to avoid military service, which will bring on its own problems. A return to the draft would pose again the vexed question of who serves when not all serve. Under peacetime force levels, only about one in three qualified males would be required for military service. Equity concerns speak against a return to a peacetime draft.

What about management steps that could be taken to improve personnel utilization within the all-volunteer framework? Most proposals in this vein do not address the core issue: getting qualified young men into the ground combat arms or onto warships. Neither lowering physical or mental standards for men, nor increasing the number of women, nor relying more greatly on civilian personnel suit the imperatives of combat assignments.

A substantial pay raise for lower enlisted personnel, another Gates Commission recommendation, was the principal rationale to induce persons to join the all-volunteer force. This has turned out to be a double-edged sword. Youth surveys show that pay motivates less-qualified youth (for example, high school dropouts, those with poor grades) to join the armed services while having a negligible effect on college bound youth. To use salary incentives as the primary motivating force to join and remain in the military can also lead to grave morale problems. If future military pay raises were to lag behind civilian scales, as now seems likely, the present grumbling throughout the career force, presently limited to perceived erosion of benefits, would become a rumbling chorus of complaint. An occupational model of the armed forces turns service members into "employees," with the recent talk of military unionization a natural by-product.

The central issue remains: is there a way without direct compulsion or excessive reliance on cash inducements to attract a cross-section of young men into the combat arms and related tasks? Or, to put it differently, is there a way we can obtain the analogue of the peacetime draftee in the all-volunteer era? I believe there is.

## Toward a Voluntary Citizen Army

One step would be a two-year enlistment option (the term of the draftee) to be restricted to the combat arms, low-skill shipboard duty, aircraft security guards, and labor-intensive jobs. The quid pro quo for such assignment would be post-service educational benefits along the lines of the G.I. Bill of World War II. College education or vocational training in exchange for two years in the combat arms would be a way to attract highly qualified soldiers who can learn quickly, serve effectively for a full tour, and then be replaced by similarly qualified recruits. Because there would be no presumption of acquiring civilian skills in the military, the terms of such short service would be honest and unambiguous, thus alleviating a major source of post-entry discontent in the all-volunteer force. The added costs of post-service educational benefits would, at least in part, be balanced by lower attrition, reduced recruitment outlays, the end of combat arms bonuses, and, most likely, fewer dependents of lower-ranking enlisted personnel.

To go a step farther, the military could set up a two-track personnel system recognizing a distinction between a "citizen soldier" and a "career soldier." ("Soldiers" as used here refers also to sailors, marines, and airmen.) The career soldier would be assigned and compensated in the manner of the prevailing system. The citizen soldier, however, would serve a two-year term in the combat arms or labor-intensive positions with low active-duty pay; few, if any, entitlements; but with deferred compensation in the form of generous post-service educational or vocational training benefits. Such benefits ought to be linked with reserve obligations following active duty. Without extensive reliance on prior-service personnel, there seems to be no way to salvage Army reserve components in the all-volunteer context.

The immediate goal is to break the mind-set that sees the all-volunteer force in terms of econometric models. Experience to date has shown that the market system is not the way to recruit an all-volunteer Army. To regard the military as an occupation also raises nagging issues on the future of the armed forces in American society. The all-volunteer force as presently constituted has come to exclude enlisted participation by those who will be America's future leaders, whether in government, business, or the intellectual and academic communities. Will enlisted service gradually become viewed as a place for those with no other options? Will the career military acquire an increasingly distorted view of American youth and civilian society? Rotating participation of middle-class youth would leaven the enlisted ranks and help reinvigorate the notion of military service as a widely shared citizen's duty. It would prevent labeling the Army as a recourse for dead-end youth, a characterization hard to escape, even if unfair, unless enlisted membership reflects a cross-section of American youth.

A more broad proposal assumes that the definition of military service needs overhauling as badly as the machinery of selection. Now is the time to consider a voluntary national service program—in which military duty is one of several options—which would be coupled with post-service educational benefits. For purposes of discussion, a two-year national service program aimed at youth—female and male—is proposed. Such service would be expected to take place between school and job, or between school and college, or between college and professional training. Voluntary servers would be compensated at levels comparable to those given draftees in the pre-Vietnam era—subsistence plus a little spending money. They would be directed toward diverse tasks that are intrinsically unamenable to sheer monetary incentives; caring for the aged falls in this category as well as serving in the combat arms. These are the very kinds of tasks that are probably best performed when not regarded as a long-term commitment. It would certainly be to the advantage of society to have such service performed by lowly paid but motivated youth. In fact, for many in their late teens and early twenties a diversion from the world of school or work would be tolerable and perhaps even welcome.

The Congress must attend to governmental policies which

undercut the all-volunteer force and the notion of citizen service. I refer to the several billion dollars a year spent on youth training programs and, most especially, to the assistance given college students in the form of federal grants or loans. It is surprising that, given the current debate on providing governmental relief for middle-class families with children in college, no public figure has thought to tie such student aid to any service obligation on the part of the youths who benefit. It is philosophically defensible as well as downright practical to hold that any able-bodied young person who did not perform national service, whether civilian or military, would be ineligible for governmental job training or student aid.

The overriding strategy is to make governmental subsidies of youth programs consistent with the ideal that citizen obligation ought to become an essential part of growing up in America. This strategy would also clarify the military's role by emphasizing the larger calling of national service.

## OPENING PANDORA'S BOX[6]

... The first tactic of the pro-draft forces—as witness Senator Stennis—has been to damn the Volunteer Army as too poor, too black, too few. This criticism, which has been fed to the public through television, network documentaries, newspapers and magazines has, of course, been on the record. Privately, the professional military and its congressional backers on the House and Senate Armed Services Committees know otherwise, as official studies and reports have documented. Thus it was when the newest detailed study ordered by Stennis's ultra-hawkish Armed Services Committee and issued December 31, 1978, under Defense Department auspices (including the Office of the Assistant Secretary of

[6] Excerpted from magazine article by Murray Polner, editor of *Present Tense* and author of *No Victory Parades: The Return of the Vietnam Veterans* and *When Can I Come Home? Commonweal.* 106:553-5. O. 12, '79. Copyright © Commonweal 1979. Reprinted by permission.

Defense for Manpower, Reserve Affairs and Logistics) concluded that "The AVF [All-Volunteer Force] has provided
the military service with a full strength active force of a quality equal to or superior to that achieved under the draft." In
an appendix to the report, two Pentagon military personnel
specialists added their own opinions, dismissing criticisms of
the Volunteer Army as merely subjective [translation: politi-
cal]: "A return to the draft is no panacea for the problems of
today's military," they wrote. "In many cases a conscripted
armed force would have even more serious problems than
today's AVF."

Nor has the remarkable achievement of the Volunteer
Army escaped the attention of Drew Middleton, military affairs specialist of the *New York Times.* The volunteers, he
conceded last March, are seen by "many commanders and
especially important, most of the noncommissioned officers
. . . as the most effective peacetime force of this century . . .
the majority of professional and noncommissioned officers
would resist a resumption of the draft."

And writing in the *Wall Street Journal* in April, William
H. Meckling, dean of the graduate school of management at
the University of Rochester and former executive director of
the President's Commission on an All-Volunteer Armed
Force, reported that the Volunteer Army is working and that
"all four of the active duty armed forces have generally been
able to maintain authorized strengths since conscription was
abolished." To claim otherwise, noted Dean Meckling, "raises
serious questions about congressional intent."

If the volunteers are doing fine, what about the charge
that our armed forces are too black? For one thing, neither
the *Times* nor Senator Sam Nunn (Dem.-Ga.) and others who
have brought up the question have explained why "too many
blacks" is not good enough. George Will, the conservative
columnist who opposes a draft, put it best by asking "So
what?" And Secretary Alexander, the first black male to hold
a cabinet position, put the matter into even sharper focus: the
ratio of black to white is "immaterial . . . I think you have to
ask . . . why there is almost 40 percent unemployment among

black teenagers before you ask why they enlist." The facts are that in 1977 the Volunteer Army had 319,000 blacks in the armed forces or 18 percent of the total number. The reason they opted for military service had nothing to do with the absence of a draft, but has mainly been because of financial rewards rather than coercion. As a result, blacks tend to reenlist, for example, in greater numbers than do whites. If the draft had been in operation, it would have had no effect whatever on the reenlistment rate of blacks and whites.

Pro-draft forces offer two additional arguments: the allegedly undermanned reserves and the costs of the Volunteer Army. So far as the first is concerned, if there actually is a shortage of reserves—and the facts are far from clear—it can be blamed on the Pentagon's mismanagement and neglect. Until August 1976 the Army had no full-time recruiting force for the reserves; they also released thousands of men and women prematurely for such reasons as "defective attitude" and "apathy." In fiscal 1976, for example, 55 percent of the recruits were let go before their tour of duty was finished. The solution for the reserves is not a draft but a good recruiting program and much improved leadership and management. All the Army would have to do to fill its ranks, insists Robert L. Nelson, the Pentagon civilian concerned with the problem, is lower its admittance standards.

Well, if it isn't the condition of the Volunteer Army, its racial composition or the state of the reserves, is it the cost? Argued Senator Nunn: "The AVF may be a luxury which we may no longer be able to afford." Yet everyone who has studied the Pentagon's expenses has discovered that retirement benefits, salaries, officers' pay and service perquisites and not the volunteers are the real reason for high personnel costs. Ex-Secretary of Defense Donald H. Rumsfeld countered the Nunn argument by pointing out that soaring costs were not due to first-term enlistments, which is all a draft would replace, and that pay raises for all first-term troops in 1977 amounted to only 18 percent of personnel costs.

In the end, the rationale for reinstituting the draft is grounded on other factors, as Drew Middleton revealed early in May as the debate heated up. The generals are calling for a draft, he wrote in the *Times*, because they believe that the "gap between the Army's global commitments and its resources is growing. This rather than the doubts about the effectiveness of the Volunteer Army, is the primary problem. These are not understood, officers say *bitterly* [my italics], by either the collegiate opposition or those in politics who adamantly oppose the resumption of the draft."

Exactly.

There are today 2.1 million men and women in uniform. Add to that number 800,000 in the Selected Reserve, 300,000 in the Individual Ready Reserve, up to 100,000 in the Delayed Entry Program, all buttressed by the largest, most destructive nuclear arsenal in history. Where is the prospect of a land war that justifies this sort of preliminary mobilization? The Soviet antagonist, while dangerous, is in truth an aging and clumsy bear, with severe internal and foreign problems, an inefficient economy, a brutal governing system, a Chinese nightmare to the east and unreliable client states to the west. Nor have the Soviets done well in the Third World where they cannot help with much more than armaments, the last thing in the world those underdeveloped nations need.

Not to be ignored is the fact that the return of registration or the draft will surely reopen the bitter divisions of the Vietnam war, a fact recognized even by the Defense Department study. Strong opposition is developing on campuses and elsewhere: organizations are being formed, resolutions passed, petitions signed, demonstrations held. Pro-draft forces are opening a Pandora's box again that had best remain closed. The latent anger of the 1960s could easily be aroused again among the children of the middle and (this time) working classes.

Yet the pro-draft forces push ahead, methodically, myopically, stubbornly. If there is a draft, there will be young men (and conceivably, this time, young women too)—18-year-old young men—who resist. Do Senators Stennis and Nunn and their cohorts really wish to force them into prison or Canadian exile? And in a time of peace? Have Senator Stennis and the other hawks who supported Vietnam escalation at every stage recognized their debt to the soldiers of the 1960s and 1970s, the Vietnam veterans who have been and continue to be treated so shabbily by their country? Are we ready to establish yet another generation of victims?

Registration leads to a draft which will inevitably lead to military adventurism. I much prefer the comment ascribed to Rep. Marjorie S. Holt (R.-Md.), a member of the House Military Personnel Subcommittee which recently voted 5–4 to support registration for men turning 18 years of age after December 31, 1980—that is, *after the elections*—who said, "People are just going to say we're silly. We're trying to bring back a peacetime draft when we don't need it."

---

## TODAY'S AMERICAN ARMY[7]

---

"The American army is not as good as it used to be, and never was." With that delphic sentence an American general recently tried to shrug off the widespread criticism of Nato's largest fighting force. Unsuccessfully: the criticism continues, from military men and politicians in both western Europe and the United States. The apologetic general was right, in a convoluted way. But he was also dangerously complacent. There is a nagging worry that this time the American army's problems are more serious and intractable than ever before, and could quickly get disastrously worse.

In sheer size, today's American army is still a formidable instrument. It has 16 combat divisions—four armoured, six mechanised, four infantry, two airborne (one helicopter and one parachute)—plus nine independent brigades and armoured cavalry regiments, each roughly equivalent to a third of a division. Five of the divisions based in the United States consist of two regular brigades plus one brigade of National

[7] Reprint of staff-written magazine article "Today's American Army," *The Economist.* 279:23–5. Ap. 25, '81. Copyright © The Economist Newspaper Ltd., London, 1981. Reprinted by permission.

Guard (ready reserve) troops. That sounds like a weakness but is not. The National Guard soldiers, although almost all part-timers, are well trained and well equipped fighting men; most of them have long service with their units. In many respects they are better than the regular soldiers they serve with.

Of this army, two armoured divisions, two mechanised ones, an air defence command of about divisional size and five independent brigades and regiments are stationed in Germany. That is the second largest force, after West Germany's, on Nato's central front. All in all, some 40% of the American army is posted outside the continental United States.

Besides the troops on the ground, the United States has weapons and equipment stockpiled in Germany for another armoured division, a mechanised one and an armoured cavalry regiment, and is in the process of bringing over enough equipment for a total of six extra divisions. The men would be flown in from the United States in the first few days of fighting (or earlier), pick up their hardware, and go to war.

### Guns okay, men less so

But would they win it? Is the quality of the equipment, and the men, up to the stress of combat? Even if it is now, will it still be so five years hence?

The equipment problem is the easier one, because money can solve it. But it will take money by the bucketful. The trouble is that a lot of new weapons, put on the drawing board in the post-Vietnam rush to catch up on postponed research and development work, are now going into production at about the same time. The main things the army wants are:
☐ new helicopters;
☐ a new tank;
☐ a new armoured personnel carrier (now a vehicle to fight from, not just ride to battle in, at a breathtaking increase in price);
☐ a new air-defence missile, Patriot, to replace both the medium-range Hawk and the long-range Nike Hercules;
☐ a mobile battlefield rocket-launcher;

☐ two new anti-aircraft tanks (one with missiles, one with guns).

Most of these things are costing more than the original estimates, some a lot more. To compound the misery, more of them are needed than had been originally planned—because of the need to stockpile for those six divisions that would be flown into Europe in a crisis. So far the equipment for this pre-stocking has mostly come out of the divisions stationed in the United States.

On top of all this, the American army's managers are avariciously eyeing the new concept of the Rapid Deployment Force, which involves the pre-positioning of equipment at bases in the Middle East or on ships in the Indian Ocean. There is a good chance that the army will make some expensively wrong choices here, such as buying a light tank to be carried in aircraft. (It would probably cost as much as a real tank, be much less efficient, and still not be light enough to be flown around in sufficient numbers to do much good.) Estimates of the total cost of the new equipment—even without new items for the Rapid Deployment Force—range from $40 billion upwards, in today's money, over the next five years.

Even so, today's American army is still the best equipped ground force in Nato, and is likely to remain so if Mr. Reagan's defence plans go through congress. The worry is about the people who carry the guns. In the seven years that the American army has been an all-volunteer force, two unpleasant things have happened.

First, the quality of recruits (as measured by written entry tests or by the percentage who are high-school or college graduates) has dropped sharply. The quality of the junior officers has also come down, in step with the general recruiting level. When the army was conscripted, large numbers of college men offered themselves as officers to avoid being drafted into the ranks, so the army could be choosey. Now there is little competition, and the army has to take what it can get. The military academy at West Point continues to turn out top-flight officers, but these are only a fraction of the total intake. Some senior officers prefer today's young officers to the "draft-dodgers" of the 1960s, who may have been brighter but were not as committed to army life as today's volunteers. Others prefer the old sort.

Second, the end of the draft has meant the virtual disappearance of the army's inactive reserves, mostly men recently released from their period of conscription (and including some who were avoiding it). These would have been the main source of reinforcements for Europe after about the first 30 days of a war.

So far the army has coped fairly well with its dimmer recruits, by giving them extra education programmes. But that means less time for military training. And even the simpler forms of military training now take longer. Thick soldiers learn slowly and forget easily. One tank company commander describes his gunnery problems:

There will never be enough time. We brief them on the qualification run, and they go through it again and again. It should take a day for a company to qualify; sometimes it takes three. Most of the crews will qualify eventually, but three months later it's like they've never seen the range before. We have to start all over from scratch.

Such repetition does not produce adaptable soldiers. During a recent Nato exercise, European officers were astonished by ineffective American camouflage techniques and questionable tactics. When questioned about them, American officers explained that this was the way they always did things—in Texas.

Soldiers of low intelligence are also less likely to finish their first engagement and less likely to re-enlist than more intelligent ones. So more new soldiers have to be trained. The result is a downward spiral of quality. The simplest solution would be to bring back the draft, but there seems little chance of that in the near future. President Reagan has said he is against it, most potential draftees are against it, and almost all senior officers are against it; its supporters are mostly outside critics of the army.

A variation to get around these difficulties is now being considered by some senior officers. This is to draft men for the reserves only, giving them around four months of active training followed by two or three years of weekend and summertime duty. It is reckoned that, in addition to strengthening the reserves, this would encourage regular enlistments.

To try to get better soldiers without the draft, the army is pinning its hopes on a "compensation package" which it plans to send to congress this spring. This will consist of sharply increased pay—not so much for new soldiers as for those who stay on for a second tour—and a new "GI bill" providing men with money to go to college when they complete their service.

The idea is to attract potential college students—which most recruits now are not—who would be better soldiers and a few of whom, attracted by the big pay rise they would get on re-enlistment, would stay in the army. Nobody is saying how much all this will cost (the college money conveniently comes from another department's budget), but it will be a bomb. Yet it could be the government's last chance to avoid going back to the draft.

### *The alternative that wasn't*

If unintelligent soldiers weren't enough of a headache, there are not enough even of them. So the army has turned to enlisting more women, which the women's rights movement had been pushing for anyway. Women now make up 8% of the army's total strength. But they have not worked out well.

Although generally brighter and less liable to get into most kinds of trouble than their male colleagues, the women have proved an unreliable lot in one inimitable way. At any given time, around 10% of any unit's women—and some units depend heavily on women—are off duty because they are pregnant or have just had a baby. The army will allow a woman to stay in after her baby comes if she can manage to take care of it and soldier at the same time. But she can get out if she chooses. Some women get pregnant just in order to be allowed to cut short their enlistment. And three out of four pregnant girl soldiers interviewed by your correspondent said that the main reason they joined the army was to have a baby at government expense.

The job of any army is to fight. There is no law in the United States that prohibits women soldiers from serving in combat. The army has so far kept them out of most of the "sharp-end" units, such as tank and infantry battalions and armed helicopters. But women are serving in other places—such as Pershing missile sites and brigade headquarters—where they would almost certainly come under fire in wartime, and might well have to fight.

It is by no means clear that women cannot fight as well as men in the 1980s, particularly if some kinds of equipment were designed with their physical requirements in mind. But the implications of using women in combat have not been faced squarely either by the army or by congress. Some male officers obviously feel threatened by the idea that women can do their jobs. But many of the more self-confident men also have serious reservations. Would the presence of women in combat areas sap the men's morale? Would they try to protect the women instead of fighting? What would their reactions be to the sight of wounded women, or mangled dead ones? No one knows, yet. But the doubts linger. The sight of a very pregnant woman in a flowered maternity dress guarding a military base—the army has only recently started to buy maternity uniforms—does not conjure up visions of a fierce and warlike fighting force.

Warlike or not, there is no longer any question of getting rid of the women. They are needed too badly, and the drive for sexual equality has gone too far; feminists have petitioned the Supreme Court to have them included in the registration for the draft. The army is going to have to figure out a way to use its women more effectively. Discharging those who become pregnant during their first enlistment, without compensation, might be a start.

### Best of the blacks, worst of the whites

Another of the army's problems is widely assumed to be its huge number of blacks—29% of the total. In fact, this is not, or not yet, a major worry.

The average black recruit today comes from the higher intellectual and social levels of the black community; the reverse is true of the average white. Two thirds of black recruits are high-school graduates; not much more than half of the whites are. The blacks are generally in better physical condition. Most of them make splendid soldiers. Many seek duty in front-line combat units. The 1st Armoured Division, one of the best divisions in Nato, is 38% black, and some of its armoured and infantry battalions have an even higher proportion of blacks. Racial frictions there are, but they are not as bad as they were five years ago. The increased number of blacks is one reason for that: they can look after themselves now.

But the problem is not measured only by troubles in the barracks. Although black soldiers fought well in mixed units in Korea and Vietnam, there are still worries about how all-black or nearly all-black units would perform in a controversial war, or against other colored soldiers. Apart from these purely military concerns, the social and political implications of an all-black army defending a 12%-black country are staggering.

One eminent sociologist thinks it could come to that. He predicts that, as the proportion of blacks grows, whites will become less likely to sign on, and somewhere along the scale there will occur a "tipping effect" that will pour all the whites out and leave a solid black army. The tipping point may not be far off.

One problem that the races seem to share is drugs: blacks and whites are equally likely to use them. Drugs have plagued the American army more than any other fighting force in modern times. During the Vietnam war widespread drug abuse was almost certainly one reason for the army's poor performance, particularly in the later years. But things are a bit better now.

The army reckons that 20% of its soldiers use some kind of drug once a month, and that 6.8% use hard drugs that often. These are still startlingly high numbers, but the level seems to be coming down, slowly. Drugs are perhaps less of a long-term threat to the army's combat performance than its manifest problem with rising alcoholism.

## *Soft-centered*

Since the end of the draft, the American army has become volunteer without becoming professional, a body apart, without being either elite or proud. The volunteer army's performance on maneuvers has failed to convince its allies—or its enemies—that it could fight a long war successfully. It is a brittle army.

The main combat units are well equipped and reasonably well trained. They could probably fight well on the day a war started. But more than that is needed. Your correspondent's judgment is that the American army is not up to the long-war job today. There is no reserve force to speak of. It would take months to bring back conscription and train conscripts. There are not enough intelligent corporals and sergeants to replace the sergeant and lieutenant casualties and at the same time provide a pool of experienced leaders to train the new men. It is not an adaptable army.

Beneath a hard surface, the core is soft and spongy. The American army's weaknesses have to be cured, soon, if it is to face the challenges of the 1980s.

## II. THE QUESTION OF REGISTRATION

### EDITOR'S INTRODUCTION

In December 1979 when the Soviet Union invaded Afghanistan the Carter administration interpreted it as a possible prelude to further Soviet inroads into the Middle East. On January 23, 1980 President Carter therefore asked Congress in his State of the Union address for the budgetary authority to begin a standby registration to "meet future mobilization needs rapidly as they arise." Two weeks later he submitted to Congress a detailed request to register during the summer both *men* and *women* turning 19 and 20 in 1980, while those turning 18 would have to register later in the year. In 1981 and thereafter each person would be required to register upon reaching their eighteenth birthday. The President reiterated his position that he saw no need at the time for a draft. With 52 Americans also held captive in Iran, he hoped that Congress would quickly approve his plan.

Congress immediately considered Carter's registration proposal. Except for the House Armed Services Personnel Subcommittee voting 8 to 1 to exclude women, both houses authorized the funding and on June 27 President Carter signed the bill.

Even with such support, President Carter did encounter some disagreement with his draft registration proposal. Both Senator Kennedy and Governor Brown of California, his two rivals for the Democratic nomination for the presidency, announced their opposition to registration. Among the Republican candidates, George Bush and John Connally supported registration, while Ronald Reagan and John Anderson opposed it.

In an interview from *U. S. News & World Report*, Senator Sam Nunn, Democrat of Georgia, argues in favor of draft registration in order to have effective emergency mobilization. "But the real probability is that at some point we either will have to return to the draft or cut substantially our overall defense commitments." Senator Mark Hatfield, Republican of Oregon, in the same interview is strongly against registration "Because registration cannot be separated from a draft; it's all part of the same program. The peacetime draft is more characteristic of a totalitarian system than of a free society."

Two draft-age Americans writing in *The Progressive* express their feelings about having to register. One chose to do so, the other refused. Christopher Garlock feels "firm in my conviction that registering was both the practical and moral course for me." On the other hand, Matthew Bunn thinks " 'Submit' is probably the most honest word in the entire Selective Service Act; registration is a *submission*, of both your body and your conscience, for use at any moment by the military machine."

The next article from *U.S. News & World Report* explains just who must register and the actual procedures for doing so at post offices throughout the United States.

In the final article, Russell Baker writing in the *New York Times Magazine* brings his inimitable point of view to the whole draft registration debate and asks "Why is this opportunity for edifying Government service limited to Government service with ammunition?"

---

## FOR DRAFT REGISTRATION[1]

Reprinted from *U.S. News & World Report*

---

*Interview with Senator Sam Nunn
Democrat, of Georgia*

*Q Senator Nunn, why do you favor resumption of registration for the draft?*

[1] Reprint of interview entitled "Should U.S. Revive the Draft?" *U.S. News & World Report.* 88:37–8. F. 11, '80.

*A* First, a basic assumption of the volunteer force was that registration would continue. The Gates Commission, which recommended the volunteer military, never envisioned that we would have no contingency plan for emergency mobilization based on a draft.

Second, it's obvious from military exercises that in an emergency we simply could not fulfill mobilization plans; we could not carry out our military mission. You can argue that perhaps the military mission should be changed. But I don't think you can logically argue that we should retain current military missions and the current manpower policies that would prevent us from fulfilling these missions.

*Q What practical effect would registration have on U.S. readiness in a serious crisis?*

*A* Registration cuts 90 to 100 days off the time needed to get young men to report for training. Without it, in an emergency it would take about 110 days before the first inductee reported. Then that individual would not be prepared for combat until receiving another three months' training.

That means about seven months would elapse before the first draftee became available for duty. In the meantime, we would completely deplete our reserve forces and be in a desperate condition because of manpower shortages in combat units. We would be faced with the choice between capitulation and early resort to nuclear weapons.

*Q Do you share the feeling that registration would make a draft all but inevitable?*

*A* I don't think it would be automatic. It is possible that registration, if implemented with a great deal of leadership, may stimulate more volunteers. But the real probability is that at some point we either will have to return to the draft or cut substantially our overall defense commitments. We are at a point where our vital interests greatly exceed our military capability to defend them—and, to me, that spells danger.

*Q What is your attitude toward the registration of women?*

*A* I vigorously oppose the registration of women because I do not believe there is any military necessity for it. I agree with the present law that prohibits women from being drafted or going into combat. If you're not going to send women into combat, there is no need to draft women. And if you're not going to draft women, there's no need to register women.

*Q Aren't women needed for noncombat jobs?*

A Women are playing a vital role as volunteers in peacetime, but the premium in wartime will be on combat-trained men. In an emergency, all of our training facilities will be needed for combat training. Even now, there is a critical shortage of training facilities for wartime contingencies.

*Q Wouldn't Moscow view registration of women as a further sign of U.S. determination?*

A If this turns into a debate on the equal rights of women and the desirability of women in combat rather than a debate on our crucial national security, we'll be sending precisely the opposite message.

We are in a grave and dangerous period. If we allow sociological issues to be the focal point, then the message sent to the Soviets will be almost a joke. Deterrence depends on America's military readiness, not on our commitment to a sociological experiment on the battlefield.

*Q Then how should the President proceed?*

A I advocate registration of males, with registration of women subject to a separate debate so that we do not hold up in any way the registration of young men. The President has the legal authority now to register males, but to register females he would have to come back to Congress—and, in my opinion, we'd have a filibuster. Those opposed to any form of registration would be joined by those who oppose the registration of women.

*Q Is there danger that a new draft would create national divisions like those during the Vietnam War?*

A The President has called for registration, not for a Vietnam-type draft. There will be strong feelings. But the President has the legal authority to resume registration. If he confines his plan to males, those who are opposed will have a very difficult battle. There will be protests around the country. But I do not believe you're going to see an overwhelming majority of any age group opposed to such a vital national-security step.

If we as a nation are not capable of distinguishing between Vietnam and the Persian Gulf, then we've got problems beyond the scope of my imagination. We had almost no economic interest in Southeast Asia, but we have a very strong economic interest in the Persian Gulf.

There is no hope that we can eliminate our substantial dependence on oil from the Persian Gulf region in the next decade. We have a vital economic interest in seeing that that oil continues to flow. If Russia gained a foothold in the Persian Gulf that allowed them to dominate the area, it would be disastrous not only for the economy of the United States but also for that of the free world.

*Q Would you be in favor of college deferments if a new draft were imposed?*

*A* We certainly should not repeat the Vietnam experience. Any deferments for students should be based on critical educational skills, such as medicine. And it should be made clear that there would be automatic entry into the military upon completion of that education. If we allow colleges to become a sanctuary, we perpetrate the same gross inequities that exist now in the volunteer force.

Middle and upper-class America are not sufficiently participating in the defense of the country today except in the officer corps. That's one of the tragedies of the volunteer force, and it portends very serious problems for our democracy.

## AGAINST DRAFT REGISTRATION[2]

Reprinted from *U.S. News & World Report*

### *Interview with Senator Mark O. Hatfield Republican, of Oregon*

*Q Senator Hatfield, why do you oppose registration for a possible draft in the future?*

A Because registration cannot be separated from a draft; it's all part of the same program. The peacetime draft is more characteristic of a totalitarian system than of a free society. It is a system of involuntary servitude.

If we had not had the draft, we would never have been at war for the length of time we were in Vietnam. As long as each President had that unlimited supply of manpower, he could sustain that policy without a congressional declaration of war.

A draft is not the proper means for responding to an international emergency. The 1.3-million reserve force is for that. They are already trained. A draft should be used only to sustain a military commitment in protracted international conflict.

Let me state the obvious: I am not a pacifist, and I am not antimilitary. But I believe that the true vulnerability of America today lies not with our lack of military manpower or arms; it lies with our massive dependence upon energy imports, our inflation and our underproductive economy.

*Q Would registration really make a draft inevitable?*

A Absolutely. I am thoroughly convinced of that. In the last five budgets, the Selective Service was prohibited from using any funds in connection with induction of any person into the armed forces.

The President's new budget seeks to delete that important check and balance that the Congress has placed upon the warmaking powers of the President.

[2] Reprint of interview entitled "Should U.S. Revive the Draft?" *U.S. News & World Report.* 88:37–8. F. 11, '80.

*Q Advocates argue that without advance registration, U.S. mobilization efforts in future crises would be impaired—*

A That is not so. The Defense Department wants the first draftee registered and processed in 30 days—ready for basic training. But the Selective Service says that even today we can beat that time schedule by five days, or have the first person ready for basic training in 25 days—without any pre-registration procedure. Under the early registration called for by the President, we would surpass that 30-day target by only 13 days.

*Q Then you see registration as a political move—*

A Certainly. It would do nothing to add to our national strength. In fact, it would be a minus. It would create dissension and problems we have not had since the 1960s. Remember, the penalty for failing to register is precisely as severe as refusal to be inducted into the military: Up to five years in prison and a $10,000 fine.

*Q Do you foresee national protests of the kind that occurred during the Vietnam War?*

A A lot depends on the foreign circumstances. If an action were designed to secure Persian Gulf oil—and only to secure oil for wasteful consumption—then a very deep division in the American public would be likely.

*Q Wouldn't registration in this country send a useful signal to the Soviet Union?*

A We can send more-effective signals without restoring the warmaking powers of the President, which Congress deliberately circumscribed after Vietnam.

*Q Is it possible to sustain the volunteer army without a draft given its high personnel costs?*

A Absolutely. Statistics prove it can be done: In 1979 the numbers of the Reserves went up. In recent weeks, the numbers of volunteers have increased considerably.

Today we have over 2 million in uniform and we have 1.3 million in the Reserves. We have a right to ask the question: What kind of commitment is the President making? What kind of foreign policy requires such an increase in our level of military manpower? Are we again to assume alone the role of world policeman?

*Q How would you propose to make up what the military claims are serious recruiting and manpower shortages?*

A I have supported and will continue to support appropriations for military-pay increases and for increased fringe benefits. I have supported the retention of men in the Reserves in the past when efforts have been made to reduce the numbers. I have consistently supported everything that could be justified to strengthen the volunteer and reserve programs.

*Q Isn't there a potential Soviet military threat facing us in the Middle East?*

A What is the national interest in the Persian Gulf? Oil—the dependency upon imported oil. But could we really secure the oil fields?

The truth is that there is no real security out there for us under any circumstances, irrespective of what the Soviet Union does. The oil supply could be cut off by internal disruptions in those countries tomorrow.

*Q Are there enough votes in the Senate to block the move for registration?*

A I'm sure we'll have sufficient numbers to make at least a parliamentary attack on it. But we don't have the majority of votes.

*Q If the draft does resume, would you be in favor of the conscription of women?*

A I don't want to draft men or women, but if we're going to have a draft, it has to be across the board. I can't support the equal-rights amendment and then pull back and say, "But it shouldn't include the draft." And if a woman is drafted, she should not be barred from the front lines.

Some good gentlemen hard-liners back off from the idea of putting females into the combat military operations.

*Q Do you have a fundamental quarrel with the concept of military service?*

A This nation was founded to serve the people, not vice versa. And to believe that we're serving the nation only when we are in uniform is completely fallacious.

A schoolteacher, a nurse, a farmer or anybody in a legitimate pursuit is serving the nation. A coercive, mandatory service to the state is one basis of totalitarianism.

## WHY I REGISTERED FOR THE DRAFT[3]

There's a feeling you get when you walk into a hospital, no matter how slight the problem to be treated—a vague, general fear of your own human frailty and a realization of helplessness once the doctors and nurses take over.

That was the feeling I experienced in July when I walked into the post office to register my name with the Selective Service System. Much thought and discussion had brought me to the post office, firm in my conviction that registering was both the practical and moral course for me.

But when the postal clerk slid the registration form in front of me, my confidence and poise slid away, leaving a naked feeling of helplessness. What was I doing there? Was I making a dreadful mistake?

Several months ago I chuckled over an editorial in *The New York Times*—not realizing how soon I would gag on my own laughter—which expressed support for registration and the draft. The thrust of the editorial was transparent—fear that the predominantly black armed forces might not be willing to defend capitalism when this country goes to war over oil.

From discussions with my father, who opposed the Vietnam war, I have learned that there was no draft resistance in the early stages of that war, when black men were being drafted and middle-class white men were able to obtain college deferments. It was only in the late 1960s, when the Gov-

[3] Reprint of magazine article by Christopher Garlock, a reporter for the Rochester *Patriot*. *The Progressive*. 44:38. O. '80. Reprinted by permission from *The Progressive*, 408 West Gorham Street, Madison, Wisconsin 53703. Copyright © 1980, The Progressive, Inc.

ernment began drafting the sons of the white middle class, that a draft-resistance movement came into being.

It seems to me that if anybody is going to be drafted this time around, everybody should be drafted.

This time, too, the thrust of the resistance has come from the white middle class. The elevation of the registration issue to a high moral and ethical plane is largely a cop-out.

Though the Government can pass and enforce its laws, it cannot force its citizens to violate their consciences in order to obey those laws. Conscience is a funny thing, though. How many of us can honestly say we have never made a compromise with conscience for one reason or another? The question then becomes where we draw the line.

When you're fighting a war, you want to choose your battlegrounds carefully. People who say that registration must be fought because the draft must be stopped before it starts are either ignorant or naive. The move toward the draft did not begin with the symbolic requirement of registration, and it will certainly not end with the actual draft.

When the U.S. Government decides to draft me to fight for the oil fields in Saudi Arabia, I'll draw up my battle plan.

But with my commitment to social change, I must consider how best the struggle can be carried forward. My abhorrence of violence, the military, and authority notwithstanding, I may be most useful inside the armed forces. Or I may decide to fight the draft every inch of the way.

That battle is still to come.

When I walked into the post office and felt that helplessness, and saw again the naked power of the Government, I was strengthened in my conviction that I must work as hard as possible to fight the misuses of that power. I know that many young men stayed away from the post offices during those last two weeks of July. I know that they, too—perhaps for the first time—felt that same sense of helplessness, and maybe that helped them to begin the long fight for themselves against the abuse of power.

## WHY I REFUSED TO REGISTER[4]

The Selective Service Act states that "it shall be the duty of every male . . . between the ages of eighteen and twenty-six . . . to present himself for, and submit to registration. . . ." On January 23, 1980, President Carter announced that the "duty" to "submit" would once again become the law of the land. As a child of 1961, I was more dismayed than buoyed by Carter's new-found "toughness."

The bizarre machinations that followed were equally dismaying. Administration officials announced that draft registration would save ninety days in an emergency, though more than a week earlier the White House had received a Selective Service System report saying it would save only seven. On January 16, Selective Service Director Bernard Rostker had called registration "redundant and unnecessary"; he later claimed he had "recommended" it to the President and said it would "substantially reduce the time it takes to mobilize." Secretary of Defense Harold Brown executed a similar about-face with true military flair.

Then Carter sent his "comprehensive" report on registration to Congress; Representative Les Aspin revealed that the original version had condemned registration, and there had been "a mad scramble while the bureaucrats rewrote the study so it would conform to Carter's speech rather than conform to what they learned from their research." Aspin then voted *for* registration. House Majority Leader Jim Wright announced he "would not allow the President to be embarrassed" on this issue; to save one man a moment's embarrassment, he would threaten thousands with jail.

In the midst of this confusion, I was forced to examine my beliefs and values more thoroughly than I ever had before. At nineteen, no one is really prepared to make a moral/political

[4] Reprint of magazine article by Matthew Bunn, an MIT undergraduate. *The Progressive.* 44:39. O. '80. Reprinted by permission from *The Progressive*, 408 West Gorham Street, Madison, Wisconsin 53703. Copyright © 1980, The Progressive, Inc.

decision that will affect the whole course of his life; no amount of education can help you see your soul. Suddenly, questions of peace and freedom became more urgent than Maxwell's equations, T.S. Eliot, or even the movie at Central Square Cinema.

The first question (and the most easily answered) involved the meaning of registration. If registration were no more than a name on a card, the command wouldn't be backed with threats of prison. Registration is part and parcel of warfare; it serves no other useful purpose. To kill another human being, or to force another to do so, is *wrong* by any civilized moral code. Is it less wrong by the tens of thousands with the approval of Congress? To participate is to accept; by signing the card, I would have given my support to a foreign policy which accepts mass murder as a useful tool.

"Submit" is probably the most honest word in the entire Selective Service Act; registration is a *submission,* of both your body and your conscience, for use at any moment by the military machine. It is a blank check to the old; when their own failures necessitate it, they will cash it in the terrible coinage of the lives of the young.

These answers to the first question prepared me for the second: What is my real duty? Senator Sam Nunn claims that all those who refuse to register are "unpatriotic." On the other hand, Thoreau said the greatest patriots "serve the state with their consciences . . . and so necessarily resist it for the most part; and they are commonly treated by it as enemies." I realized that if I really opposed the draft, it was my duty to disobey. No system was ever toppled by cooperation. Even a conscientious objector has accepted the system's right to decide who can and who cannot be forced to kill. This is more than I feel willing to accept; as Gandhi said, "He who is a passive spectator of crime is really, and in law, an active participator in it."

Many readers may feel this is merely the impetuosity of a hot-headed child—and it may be. But idealism is a strength of youth, not a weakness, and it is a natural obstacle the draft must overcome.

The last and most difficult question has yet to be answered: Do I have the courage to carry this duty through? In February, I took the first step, announcing at a rally that I would refuse to register. The crowd roared, but I felt strangely queasy. I don't know whether I have what it takes to endure a prison term; the only answer is waiting for me in a cell.

---

## HOW NEW DRAFT REGISTRATION RULES WORK[5]

Reprinted from *U.S. News & World Report*

---

*With Senate approval on June 12, following earlier passage by the House, registration of draft-age youths now is virtually assured. Just what will registration consist of at this time?*

As proposed by President Carter and approved by Congress, each eligible youth must fill out a brief form at any one of the 34,000 U.S. post offices. Forms call for name, address, phone number, date of birth and Social Security number.

*Who must register?*

At first, only young men age 19 or 20—those who were born in 1960 and 1961. Women are exempt under the plan approved by Congress. After Jan. 1, 1981, all young men will be required to register on or about their 18th birthdays.

*Is this registration program being challenged?*

Yes. The American Civil Liberties Union plans to file a court suit after the registration bill is signed by the President, declaring the program to be unconstitutional because it applies only to men and not to women.

*When is the first group of youths supposed to register?*

Dates will be announced by the Selective Service System through newspapers, radio and TV. Sign-up periods will be spread over two weeks, one for 19-year-olds and another for 20-year-olds.

[5] Reprint of staff-written magazine article. *U.S. News & World Report.* 88:45. Je. 23, '80.

*Will those who register get draft cards?*

No. Each youth will receive a letter that confirms his registration. However, no draft cards will be issued at this time.

*Will those signing up get physical exams to see if they are eligible for some future draft?*

No. Registration will only provide a list of names and addresses of draft-age American males. It will not involve physical exams or the collection of data for determining whether a youth would be eligible for deferment or exemption from the draft.

*Then what's the purpose of the registration system?*

Largely, to save time in case of a future crisis. Congress was assured by the administration that such a registration of names could save "as many as 90 to 100 days" in the event of a military-mobilization emergency. The move also is expected to "speed the revitalization of the Selective Service and allow it to work out registration problems in peacetime."

*What will registration cost?*

About 13 million dollars, to pay for several million forms and publicity releases to newspapers and radio/TV stations, plus some additional staff for the present standby Selective Service system. This is on top of the regular Selective Service budget of 7.8 million. Actual processing of the registration forms will be done on keypunch computers of other agencies of the federal government. The cost of starting up a peacetime draft again—should it be voted later—would run into several hundreds of millions of dollars a year.

*Suppose a youth is clearly draft exempt because of a physical disability—does he still have to register?*

Yes. Everyone in the specified age group has to register, except members of the active armed forces.

*What is the penalty for youths who fail to register?*

By law, the penalty is a fine of $10,000 and up to five years in prison for willfully failing to sign up. There has been no indication yet as to how closely those who defy the order might be prosecuted in peacetime. Those who register and fail to report when they change their addresses will be "subject to prosecution for a felony" under the program.

*Now that registration has congressional approval, can the President start up the draft again?*

Not without the express approval of Congress. In case of a national emergency calling for mobilization, the plan is for the White House to ask Congress immediately to authorize a call-up of draftees, then for Selective Service boards to quickly start processing the registrants and acting on requests for exemptions or deferments.

*On what grounds might exemptions or deferments be granted?*

Basically, the acceptable grounds would be physical or mental disabilities, hardship situations or conscientious objection.

*In case the draft is reinstated, who will be the first to go?*

Young men who are in their 20th year. Within that group of 20-year-olds, the priority for being called up will be fixed by a lottery operated by the Selective Service, which selects the order of each date of birth out of the 365 days of that year.

*Just how long after registration would it take to start actual drafting?*

The first draftees could begin arriving at military-training centers within two weeks after Congress gives its O.K., Selective Service officials believe. Within a month after mobilization day, the induction system could be working at maximum capacity, and about 100,000 draftees could be processed. Six months after the mobilization call, as many as 650,000 could be called up.

*How many young men will be registered now?*

Under the approved plan, Selective Service expects to register the names and addresses of 4 million American males in coming weeks and another 2 million next January, when the 18-year-olds register. After that, it will register about 2 million each year. If the law were changed to register women later, it would about double the number of young Americans involved.

*How long has it been since Americans were registered for the draft?*

A little more than five years, ever since President Ford

put a halt to draft registration in March, 1975. Actually, drafting ended in this country on Dec. 31, 1972.

## THE DRAFT[6]

Speaking of the draft, have you ever wondered why the only branch of Government that has to conscript labor is the military?

Nobody ever argues for drafting people into the State Department, or the Federal Power Commission, or the F.B.I. And what about the office of the President? It needs more people every year, but nobody ever says, "Let's have Selective Service send out a bunch of letters saying, 'Greetings: You are ordered to report for two years' duty at the White House.'"

And the Congress—it always needs elevator operators, doorkeepers, people to do the piping and greet the folks from back home. Does Congress ever say, "Let's draft young Americans for these jobs?" You bet your bottom dollar it doesn't.

It's only the military jobs that excite Congress's appetite for conscript labor, and of course Congressmen make a good deal of sense when they talk about why young people ought to be made to serve their country. There are good reasons for asking everybody to do a little service to the state.

It's good experience for the young. Throws them into challenging new problems, gets them out in the world where they can meet all kinds of people from all over, helps them grow and understand the complexity of the country, makes them smarter citizens who'll strengthen the political system. How can anybody who cares about the health of the country be against it?

In fact, it's such a fine way of getting young people in-

---

[6] Reprint of magazine article by Russell Baker, columnist, *New York Times. New York Times Magazine.* p 12. Jl. 27, '80. © 1980 by The New York Times Company.

volved in the country's problems that you wonder why it's used only to fill military jobs. A lot of people with no particular interest in maintaining war equipment might be happy to register for a draft anyhow if they knew there was a chance of being drafted for work that interested them more than warfare.

As things are now, though, all they have to look forward to is the uniformed bureaucracy. This takes the edge off the excitement when the mailman brings the letter from Selective Service, since there is no chance of opening it and finding that you're going to the White House, or the State Department, or the Capitol of the United States to move those famous senators up and down in those private elevators.

Right away you know you're going to be put into uniform and taught the difference between Parade Rest and To the Rear March. Why is this opportunity for edifying Government service limited to Government service with ammunition?

One reason is that all the other jobs in which a young American can serve his country are locked up by volunteers who would be furious if they were replaced by draftees. One reason they would be furious is that most of them are earning very good salaries.

A couple of recent economic studies show that civilian Government jobs paid better wages than comparable jobs in private industry. There can be a lot of satisfaction in serving your country when you realize  that if you weren't serving your country you'd be eating a little lower on the hog.

In any case, once you get beyond the military, there is so much competition for Government jobs that there are no jobs left over in which young Americans can enjoy the healthy benefits of serving their country.

Well, you may say, if that is the case, why not raise military salaries as high as the Government's civilian salaries? Wouldn't that drain a lot of the civilian work force away from the State Department and White House and Senate elevators and leave openings for some draftees to fill a lot of these white-collar jobs?

If you ask these questions it's because you haven't thought

things through. In the first place, if you raised military salaries as high as civilian salaries, you'd have skilled workmen from the private sector pouring into the military jobs so fast they would all be filled before the white-collar Government people could apply for transfers. In the second place, the Federal payroll would go so high that taxes would be even more bankruptive than they are now, which is possible, believe it or not.

The only way to maintain the military work force without going broke is to keep salaries down, and if the pay doesn't attract the necessary labor, the solution is to draft labor which will work at unattractive wages or be court-martialed.

When things come to this pass, explanations about the rewards of serving your country are likely to seem a bit hollow. You are likely to develop the sour suspicion that you have been pressed into involuntary servitude to fill the Government's need for labor at substandard wages.

This nasty situation can be avoided and youth's need to do some service to the country can be satisfied quite sensibly by lowering salaries throughout the Government, thus inspiring many civilian workers to seek jobs in the private sector and opening work opportunities for youthful draftees in all the diverse and fascinating Government jobs at Washington's disposal.

There are nearly three million reasons why this will not be done. They are the Government's civilian employees who know why draftees are unfit to perform complex Government jobs, except in the military.

# III. FOR A MILITARY DRAFT

## EDITOR'S INTRODUCTION

President Carter's draft registration proposal unleashed a full-scale national debate over whether a draft was needed in peacetime. In his message on the State of the Union he had stated: "I believe that our volunteer forces are adequate for current defense needs and I hope that it will not become necessary to impose a draft. However, we must be prepared for that possibility."

Advocates for a draft had hoped that registration would lead immediately to a draft. Citing what they perceived to be various failures of the volunteer Army, including serious manpower shortages and a declining recruitment pool, coupled with expanding Soviet military activity and continuing turmoil in the Mideast, proponents thought a return to a draft was long overdue.

Former Army Chief of Staff and Commanding General in Vietnam, William C. Westmoreland strongly advocates its resumption. He disagrees with economists and others, including President Reagan, who think that increases in pay would be a solution to current manpower deficiencies in the military. In the first article, an interview with *U.S. News & World Report,* General Westmoreland states "The idea of competing for soldiers in the marketplace is impractical . . . Can you imagine paying private soldiers $25,000 a year?" In addition, he feels "The idea of rights has been overemphasized to the point where we have eclipsed the duties of citizenship." He would like to see a return to the patriotic concept of service to one's country.

In the second article, drawing on his memories as a Harvard college student with draft deferment during the Vietnam War, James Fallows, Washington editor of *Atlantic,* reluctantly concludes that a draft is the only equitable form of military service. We now have "a black and brown army defending a mainly white nation . . . Such a selective bearing of the burden has destructive spiritual effects in a nation based on the democratic creed."

Calling the volunteer Army an "unmitigated disaster," James Webb writing in *Atlantic* asserts it consists of those "who have been economically conscripted to do society's dirty work, as surely as if there were the most inequitable draft imaginable." He goes on to state: "our greatest need is to . . . stop being afraid to ask the men of Harvard to stand alongside the men of Harlem, same uniform, same obligations, same country."

In the next article from *Fortune,* Juan Cameron points out that "The most skilled military people—computer operators, electronic technicians, doctors, pilots, nuclear engineers—are those that are hardest to retain." The chief reason is the much higher salaries paid by private industry. The director of personnel for the Air Force claims that in the mid-1970s alone his service lost almost 400 pilots a year to the airlines. "Only a draft can solve many of the manpower problems now facing the military."

"If America is to remain faithful to its social values and its military commitments, it can no longer rely upon the 'forces of the marketplace' to meet its military manpower requirements," concludes Richard A. Gabriel writing in *America.*

---

## WHY U.S. MUST RETURN TO THE DRAFT[1]

Reprinted from *U. S. News & World Report*

---

*Q General Westmoreland, in your judgment, can this country maintain an effective Army based on voluntary recruiting?*

*A* I think we're in deep trouble as a result of the volun-

---

[1] Excerpted from an interview with General William C. Westmoreland (ret.), formerly Commanding General, U.S. Army (Vietnam) and Chief of Staff, U.S. Army. *U.S. News & World Report.* 88:36. My. 12, '80.

teer system. All along, I have felt that ending the draft and dismantling the Selective Service machinery were untimely and unwise actions. We're in deep trouble because of the tremendous political difficulties of changing the present system.

*Q What's wrong with the volunteer system?*

A The idea of competing for soldiers in the marketplace is impractical. Take the example of a point man in a rifle squad. He has what is perhaps the most hazardous job you can find. You need a young man with a lot of gumption, daring and dedication. To buy that on the marketplace is, I think, unwise and totally impractical. It could cost as much as a steeplejack. Can you imagine paying private soldiers $25,000 a year?

*Q How do you answer the argument that the volunteer system would work fine if it had more money?*

A I know the argument well. I've heard it made by Milton Friedman, the Nobel Prize-winning economist. He believes that the military should be placed on a strictly commercial basis, letting the law of supply and demand govern the recruiting of manpower. Milton Friedman is a brilliant economist, but he knows little about the military. He doesn't comprehend that a major motivation of Americans who have fought in all the wars since the Revolution has been service to country. And in between wars, a major motivation among those who served was a feeling that they were discharging an obligation of citizenship.

Those of us who pursued a military career—as many of our fathers and grandfathers before us—were motivated by a sense of service. It wasn't a job. You didn't go in to make money. You never thought about competing with your counterparts in industry. You didn't expect to have pay scales that would compete.

As long as we pursue this policy of trying to compete in the marketplace for military manpower, we are also going to fuel inflation.

*Q Do you mean that a return to the draft is imperative to maintain effective forces?*

A That is my conclusion. We need what I would call a zero draft. The draft would be on the books as an inducement to encourage men to enlist in the active forces as well as the reserves.

By terminating the draft and abolishing Selective Service machinery, we passed a message to the young people that the rules are changed: Service and dedication are no longer important. Therefore, they have no obligations. The idea of rights of citizenship has been overemphasized to the point where we have eclipsed the duties of citizenship. Rights, rights, rights, rights—that's all we've heard about the last decade. We've heard nothing about duties, nothing about responsibilities of citizenship.

*Q How would a zero-draft Army work?*

*A* It would be based on a lottery system. A young man who drew a high lottery number would have several options: He could join the National Guard or the Reserves and, after basic training, serve at home. This would insure that the National Guard and Reserves were at full strength. Or he could join the active Army as a volunteer for three years and get his choice of a variety of assignments. Or he could get drafted.

With that type of inducement, there would be comparatively few men actually drafted. Also, you would attract a cross section of the society. The present system is forcing the responsibility for the manning of our military services—the manning of the ramparts of our nation—on the underprivileged segments of our society in totally disproportionate numbers. This is sociologically and politically unsound, and I think we will rue the day we adopted the volunteer system.

It is unsound militarily because the services are being forced to lower their standards progressively to get the numbers they need. Actually, they should be raising their standards because of the sophistication of materiel. It is unwise economically because 60 percent or more of the defense budget will have to be devoted to personnel costs.

*Q Wouldn't you have to pay soldiers a reasonable wage even with this zero-draft Army scheme?*

*A* In the first two years of service, soldiers, in my opinion, should get the minimum wage. They're apprentices. But then, if they decide to become careerists, they should get a good boost in pay. Incidentally, I have encountered few men who did not benefit, by their own admission, from a tour of military service.

## WHY THE COUNTRY NEEDS IT[2]

I am more than angry. I did not give birth to my one and only son to have him snatched away from me 18 years later. My child has been loved and cared for and taught right from wrong and *will not* be fed into any egomaniac's war machine.

Our 18- to 25-year-olds have not brought this world to its present sorry state. Men over the age of 35, down through the centuries, have brought us here, and we women have been in silent accord.

Well, this is one woman, one mother, who says *no*. I did not go through the magnificent agony of childbirth to have that glorious young life snuffed out.

Until the presidents, premiers, supreme rulers, politburos, senators and congressmen of the world are ready to physically, as opposed to verbally, lead the world into combat, they can bloody well forget my child.

*Unite mothers!* Don't throw your sons and daughters away. Sometime, somewhere, women have just got to say *no*.

*No. No. No. No. No. Never my child.*

—Louise M. Saylor

(Letter published in the Washington *Post*, January 28, 1980.)

Nor my child, Mrs. Saylor. Nor either of my mother's sons when, ten years ago, both were classified I-A. But *whose*, then? As our statesmen talk again of resisting aggression and demonstrating our will—as they talk, that is, of sending someone's sons (or daughters) to bear arms overseas—the only fair

[2] Reprint of magazine article by James Fallows, Washington editor of the *Atlantic* and author of *National Defense*. 245:44–7. Ap. '80. Copyright © 1980, by The Atlantic Monthly Company, Boston, Mass. Reprinted with permission.

and decent answer to that question lies in a return to the draft.

I am speaking here not of the health of the military but of the character of the society the military defends. The circumstances in which that society will choose to go to war, the way its wars will be fought, and its success in absorbing the consequent suffering depend on its answer to the question: Whose sons will go?

History rarely offers itself in lessons clear enough to be deciphered at a time when their message still applies. But of all the hackneyed "lessons" of Vietnam, one still applies with no reservations: that we wound ourselves gravely if we flinch from honest answers about who will serve. During the five or six years of the heaviest draft calls for Vietnam, there was the starkest class division in American military service since the days of purchased draft deferments in the Civil War. Good intentions lay at the root of many of these inequities. The college-student deferment, the various "hardship" exemptions, Robert McNamara's plan to give "disadvantaged" youngsters a chance to better themselves in the military, even General Hershey's intelligence test to determine who could remain in school—all were designed to allot American talent in the most productive way. The intent was to distinguish those who could best serve the nation with their minds from those who should offer their stout hearts and strong backs. The effect was to place the poor and the black in the trenches (and later in the coffins and the rehabilitation wards), and their "betters" in colleges or elsewhere far from the sounds of war. I speak as one who took full advantage of the college-student deferment and later exploited the loopholes in the physical qualification standards that, for college students armed with a doctor's letter and advice from the campus draft counseling center, could so easily be parlayed into the "unfit for service" designation known as a I-Y. Ask anyone who went to college in those days how many of his classmates saw combat in Vietnam. Of my 1200 classmates at Harvard, I know of only two, one of them a veteran who joined the class late. The records show another fifty-five in the reserves, the stateside Army, or military service of some other kind. There may be more; the alumni lists are not complete. See how this compares with the Memorial Roll from a public high school in a big city or a West Virginia hill town.

For all the talk about conflict between "young" and "old" that the war caused, the lasting breach was among the young. In the protest marches on the Pentagon and the Capitol, students felt either scorn for or estrangement from the young soldiers who stood guard. What must the soldiers have felt about these, their privileged contemporaries, who taunted them so? To those who opposed the war, the ones who served were, first, animals and killers; then "suckers" who were trapped by the system, deserving pity but no respect; and finally invisible men. Their courage, discipline, and sacrifice counted for less than their collective taint for being associated with a losing war. A returned veteran might win limited redemption if he publicly recanted, like a lapsed Communist fingering his former associates before the HUAC [House Un-American Activities Committee]. Otherwise, he was expected to keep his experiences to himself. Most veterans knew the honor they had earned, even as they knew better than anyone else the horror of the war. They came to resent being made to suppress those feelings by students who chose not to join them and who, having escaped the war without pain, now prefer to put the whole episode in the past. Perhaps no one traversed that era without pain, but pain of the psychic variety left arms, legs, life intact and did not impede progress in one's career. For people of my generation—I speak in the narrow sense of males between the ages of twenty-eight and thirty-six or thirty-seven—this wound will never fully heal. If you doubt that, sit two thirty-two-year-olds down together, one who served in Vietnam and one who did not, and ask them to talk about those years.

At least there was theoretical consistency between what the students of those days recommended for others and what they did themselves. Their point was that no one should go to war, starting with them. It should also be said that their objection to the war, at least in my view, was important and right. And while they—we—may have proven more effective and determined in acts of individual salvation than in anything else, they at least paid lip service to the idea of the "categorical imperative," that they should not expect others to bear a burden they considered unacceptable for themselves.

I hear little of that tone in the reaction to President Carter's muted call for resumption of draft registration. Within a week of his request in the State of the Union address, I spent time at two small colleges. At both, the sequence of questions was the same. Why is our defense so weak? When will we show the Russians our strength? *Isn't it terrible about the draft?*

Senator Kennedy, who so often decried the unfairness of the draft during Vietnam, won cheers from his college audience for his opposition to draft registration, in the same speech in which he suggested beefing up our military presence in the Persian Gulf. Kennedy did go on to argue that we should not shed blood for oil, which is more than most antidraft groups have done to date. It would have been reassuring to hear the students say that they oppose registration *because* they oppose a military showdown in the Persian Gulf. Instead many simply say, We don't want to go. I sense that they—perhaps all of us—have come to take for granted a truth so painful that few could bear to face it during Vietnam: that there will be another class of people to do the dirty work. After seven years of the volunteer Army, we have grown accustomed to having suckers on hand.

That the volunteer Army is another class can hardly be denied. The Vietnam draft was unfair racially, economically, educationally. By every one of those measures, the volunteer Army is less representative still. Libertarians argue that military service should be a matter of choice, but the plain fact is that service in the volunteer force is too frequently dictated by economics. Army enlisted ranks E1 through E4—the privates and corporals, the cannon fodder, the ones who will fight and die—are 36 percent black now. By the Army's own projections, they will be 42 percent black in three years.

When other "minorities" are taken into account, we will have, for the first time, an army whose fighting members are mainly "non-majority," or, more bluntly, a black and brown army defending a mainly white nation. The military has been an avenue of opportunity for many young blacks. They may well be first-class fighting men. They do not represent the nation.

Such a selective bearing of the burden has destructive spiritual effects in a nation based on the democratic creed. But its practical implications can be quite as grave. The effect of a fair, representative draft is to hold the public hostage to the consequences of its decisions, much as children's presence in the public schools focuses parents' attention on the quality of the schools. If citizens are willing to countenance a decision that means that *someone's* child may die, they may contemplate more deeply if there is the possibility that the child will be theirs. Indeed, I would like to extend this principle even further. Young men of nineteen are rightly suspicious of the congressmen and columnists who urge them to the fore. I wish there were a practical way to resurrect the provisions of the amended Selective Service Act of 1940, which raised the draft age to forty-four. Such a gesture might symbolize the desire to offset the historic injustice of the Vietnam draft, as well as suggest the possibility that, when a bellicose columnist recommends dispatching American forces to Pakistan, he might also realize that he could end up as a gunner in a tank.

Perhaps the absence of World War II-scale peril makes such a proposal unrealistic; still, the columnist or congressman should have to contemplate the possibility that his son would be there, in trench or tank. Under the volunteer Army that possibility will not arise, and the lack of such a prospect can affect behavior deeply. Recall how, during Vietnam, protest grew more broad-based and respectable when the graduate school deferment was eliminated in 1968. For many families in positions of influence, the war was no longer a question of someone else's son. How much earlier would the war have ended had college students been vulnerable from the start?

Those newly concerned families were no better and no worse than other people at other times; they were responding to a normal human instinct, of the sort our political system is designed to channel toward constructive ends. It was an instinct that Richard Nixon and Henry Kissinger understood very well, as they deliberately shifted the burden of the war off draftees and finally off Americans, to free their hands to pursue their chosen course. Recall how fast protest ebbed with the coming of the volunteer Army and "Vietnamization" in the early 1970s. For this reason, the likes of Nixon and Kissinger might regard a return to the draft as a step in the wrong direction, for it would sap the resolve necessary for a strong foreign policy and introduce the weakening element of domestic dissent. At times leaders must take actions that seem heartless and unfair, and that an informed public would probably not approve. Winston Churchill let Coventry be bombed, because to sound the air-raid sirens and save its citizens would have tipped off the Germans that Britain had broken their code. But in the long run, a nation cannot sustain a policy whose consequences the public is not willing to bear. If it decides not to pay the price to defend itself, it will be defenseless. That is the risk of democracy.

What kind of draft? More than anything else, a *fair* one, with as few holes as possible to wriggle through. The 1971 Selective Service Act, passed when the heavy draft calls had already ended, theoretically closed most of the loopholes. But if real trouble should begin, those nine-year-old patches might give way before political pressures unless we concentrate again on the mechanics of an equitable draft. "Fairness" does not mean that everyone need serve. This year 4.3 million people will turn eighteen, 2.2 million women and 2.1 million men. For the last few years, the military has been taking 400,-000 people annually into the volunteer Army—or, in raw figures, only one in ten of the total available pool. Using today's mental and physical standards, the military knocks off 30 percent of the manpower pool as unqualified, and it excludes women from combat positions. When these calculations are combined with the diminishing number of young men—only

1.6 million men will turn eighteen in 1993—the military projects that it will need to attract one of every three "qualified and available men" by the end of the 1980s.

Read another way, this means that a draft need affect *no more* than one in three—and probably far fewer. To make the draft seem—and be—fair, the pool of potential draftees should be as large as possible, even if only a few will eventually be picked. Those who are "disabled" in the common meaning of that term—the blind, paraplegics—should be excluded, but not the asthmatics and trick-back cases who are perfectly capable of performing non-combat military jobs. The military's physical requirements now assume that nearly all men must theoretically be fit for combat, even though only 14 percent of all male soldiers hold combat jobs. The proportion of draftees destined for combat would probably be higher, since those are the positions now most understrength; if actual fighting should begin it would be higher still. But combat will never represent the preponderance of military positions, and its requirements should not blindly dictate who is eligible for the draft. Instead, everyone without serious handicap should be eligible for selection by lottery—men and women, students and non-students. Once the lottery had determined *who* would serve, assignments based on physical classifications could determine where and how.

The question of women's service is the most emotionally troubling aspect of this generally emotional issue, but the progress of domestic politics over the last ten years suggests that the answer is clear. If any sexual distinctions that would deny a woman her place as a construction worker or a telephone pole climber have been forbidden by legislators and courts, what possible distinction can spare women the obligation to perform similar functions in military construction units or the Signal Corps? President Carter recognized this reality in deciding to include women in his initial draft registration order. If women are drafted, they have an iron-clad case for passage of the Equal Rights Amendment. If they are not, their claim for equal treatment elsewhere becomes less compelling. At the same time, it is troubling to think of women in combat, or of mothers being drafted, and a sensible draft law would have to recognize such exceptions.

There should be no educational deferments except for students still in high school, and possibly in two other cases. One would be for college students who enroll in ROTC; like their counterparts in the service academies, they would be exchanging four years of protected education for a longer tour of duty as an officer after graduation. The other exception might be for doctors, possessors of a skill the military needs but cannot sensibly produce on its own. If potential doctors wanted to be spared all eligibility for the draft, they could enter a program like the Navy's V-12 during World War II, in which they could take a speeded-up college course and receive a publicly subsidized medical education, after which they would owe several years' service as military doctors. Except in the most far-fetched situations, "hardship" cases should be taken care of by compensation rather than by exemption. If these are permitted, they become an invitation to abuse: who can forget George Hamilton pleading hardship as his mother's sole supporting son? Instead, the government should offset hardship with support payments to the needy dependents.

One resists the idea of lottery, because it adds to the system the very element of caprice and unfairness it is so important to remove. But since only a fraction of those eligible to serve are actually required, there seems no other equitable way to distribute the burden. With a well-established lottery, every male and female might know at age eighteen whether he or she was near the top of the list and very likely to be called, or near the bottom and almost certainly protected. How far the draft calls went down the list would depend on how many people volunteered and how many more were needed.

None of these concerns and prescriptions would matter if the volunteer Army were what it so often seemed in the last few years—a stand-in, a symbol, designed to keep the machinery running and the troops in place, not to be sent into action for any cause less urgent than absolute survival. But now we hear from every quarter that the next decade will be a time of testing, that our will and our strategy and our manpower will be on the line. The nature of this challenge, and the style of our response, are what we should be thinking and talking about now. Our discussions will never be honest, nor our decisions just, as long as we count on "suckers" to do the job.

## WHY THE ARMY NEEDS IT[3]

. . . Something is gone from today's military, and the screams for more pay and better hardware are only symptomatic of deeper, more harmful wounds that the political process has inflicted on our ability to defend our way of life. In the one generation when we were the most enlightened and powerful nation on earth (and I use the past tense advisedly on both counts), we seemed to recognize easily the nexus between military preparedness against external threat and the creativity and freedom we enjoyed internally. Vietnam, unfortunately, muddied our logic. We exhausted ourselves on vehement, internecine arguments over whether Vietnam could in some way be defined as an "external threat" to our existence. We ignored such measurable Soviet moves as the takeover of Czechoslovakia and the expansion of their naval presence into the Mediterranean and the Indian Ocean. We came to blame the military for the Vietnam involvement, and for the ultimate failure of war itself.

Westmoreland lost the war; no matter that Lyndon Johnson once boasted that the military "couldn't bomb a shithouse" without his own approval. "The racial horrors of the military" became a byword; no matter that the military was the first institution in this society to become fully integrated,

---

[3] Excerpted from magazine article by James Webb, former Vietnam infantry commander and author of the novels *Fields of Fire* and *A Sense of Honor*. *Atlantic*. 245:34–44. Ap. '80. Copyright © 1980, by The Atlantic Monthly Company, Boston, Mass. Reprinted with permission.

and no matter that the racial problems it faced were being experienced in much more violent form in civilian society. Vietnam supposedly symbolized the ultimate collision in the "generation gap," with old and young facing each other on opposite sides of the issue; no matter that Gallup polls showed that the most consistent support for the war came from those under the age of thirty.

Lacking any clearly defined external threat, the military became the threat. And, lacking a clearly defined mission, it became a very convenient sociological lab for political experimentation. Project 100,000 (which eventually became Project 400,000) was designed to test whether mental rejects could function as soldiers. When it was discovered that by and large they could not, the military was blamed for the failure. In another context, politicians and judges decided that their judgment, albeit removed, was more accurate than that of military commanders at the scene as to what sort of performance went into "honorable service." The military discharge system, they maintained, was unfair and stigmatizing; no matter that the military during Vietnam awarded 97 percent of its people discharges under honorable conditions, more than 93 percent of them with full honorable discharges, which is a more successful matriculation rate than that of any other large institution in this country.

As the military began to come unglued because of such intense political meddling, it was often blamed for that, too. Books such as the much-lauded *Crisis in Command* [Hill & Wang, '78] claim that a failure of leadership created the military's difficulties, with no mention of political overcontrol and its effect on the erosion of discipline.

. . . I recall my first summer of sea duty, at the very dawn of the Vietnam War, as we shuttled men and weapons to Hawaii on their way to the war zone. We would stand in the mess hall lines, a hundred men conversing or reading from ever-present paperback books that fit neatly in the rear pockets of our dungarees, and it was a chilling deterrent when the call went down the line, "Gangway! Prisoners! Gangway! Prisoners!" We would move against one wall and the Marine guards would march the prisoners past us, to the front of the line. Their heads would be shaved and their hats would be turned upside-down over their onion heads and they would walk in one rank, so close that each man's nose was pushed into the back of the head of the man in front of him. They could neither look nor talk except, as they picked up silverware and plates and food, to gain permission from the security guard each time they moved even a hand. "One knife, sir? One spoon, sir?" They ate in an isolated space behind the chow line, away from the other sailors and marines, sitting at attention and requesting permission to take each bite. At four o'clock every morning, the marines brought them up to the chilly, wind-blown flight deck and ran them. It was no fun to be in the brig, but those who broke regulations were on full notice about what awaited them. And the visible display of those sanctions was a measurably effective deterrent: I never saw more than perhaps eight men in the prisoner line, on a ship of several thousand sailors.

Today, such treatment would constitute a violation of individual rights. At the same time, the Navy's absentee and desertion rates over the past three years have been the highest in its history. The connection is absolute: military men don't run away from discipline, they run away when there is no discipline.

I thought of those shaved prisoners recently when I read a story in the Baltimore *Sun* about five soldiers at the Army Ordnance Center at Aberdeen, Maryland, who had repeatedly refused to get a regulation haircut. Their heads were shaved down to crewcut level as a punishment, after the soldiers were given the option of having such haircuts administered to them or undergoing an Article 15 disciplinary hearing. The soldiers then decided to complain that their rights had been violated. The end result: the company commander, the first sergeant, and the sergeant who administered the haircuts were relieved of their duties.

The soldiers, according to an Army spokesman, "said they felt they have been satisfied with the action taken." The Army spokesman did not comment on whether the company commander and his NCO's were satisfied with it.

Nor did the Army or anyone else seem to wonder about

the effect on a unit when its members learn they can violate regulations, not only with impunity, but at the direct expense of those charged with upholding the regulations. One clear indication that such destruction of traditional discipline affects military performance comes from the very unit in which this incident occurred. The soldiers were trainees in the command's automotive trade course, which supposedly prepares enlistees to maintain and repair mechanized equipment. An extensive behavioral study conducted by the Army in 1978, directed by Brigadier General Frederick Brown, found that only 45 percent of the E2 and E3 automotive repairmen in the Army's operating units could perform even 1.3 of the eight "common maintenance tasks" designed to keep their equipment functioning on a daily basis. The study further found that only 30 percent of the E4 and E5 track vehicle mechanics could perform 1.1 of their eight basic tasks.

Discipline in training develops an individual's attitudes toward the military and toward himself as a soldier. Greater discipline in the initial stages of a marine's service life is the most marked reason the Marine Corps has traditionally been able to take the same street dude or farmer that the Army might draw on and make him a much better fighting man. Contrarily, as in the present Army, when discipline disappears, so does an individual's perception that he is learning and performing tasks that go beyond what he would be doing in the civilian world.

Somehow, we seem to have lost that perception. We have built the essential elements of defeat into our military, preprogrammed many units for failure because of political fantasies. Our soldiers cannot even maintain their equipment under nonstressful situations, and we relieve commanders who attempt to develop a sense of discipline in those responsible for the equipment. We may well need better pay and newer equipment, but our most urgent need is more discipline and fewer political intrusions.

Gather a group of military professionals in a room where they believe they are among their own and you hear bitter, laconic tales, told with a sense of powerlessness and even doom. Of the military commander during the *Mayaguez* incident issuing an order and hearing the heavy German tones of Kissinger cutting through the tactical net, countering his command from 10,000 miles away, two decades of preparation for that very moment negated by a politician watching a tote board in Washington. Of variations on that theme played daily in Vietnam, until it was a litany. Of a present administration so dominated by internationalism on one hand and domestic politics on the other that it sees the military as a domestic political tool, and is more consumed with how many women it can put into a tank than with whether the tanks are operable. Of federal judges who dare to say that voluntary heroin use, which threatened to shut down many operating units several years ago, and which is a federal crime in the civilian world, nonetheless constituted service that is deserving of a mandatory honorable discharge. Of a Congress that is more afraid of the protests of a few thousand comfortable college students than it is of the reality that our manpower situation has deteriorated to the point where our reserves, which are the linchpin of any future mobilization, are three quarters of a million men understrength. Our active duty military will be stranded in a future conflict. We need the draft back.

The last cut is the deepest, because it demonstrates to the military professional that his life is considered less important than someone else's political career. The volunteer Army, which is repeatedly referred to as "only a peacetime Army" by Department of Defense politicians, was designed to operate as part of a triad, alongside a strong reserve and a Selective Service system that remained able to draft citizens on short notice. Both of these backups have been eviscerated to the point where they would contribute little in a mobilization.

Selective Service is in "deep standby." DOD mobilization plans call for delivering the first contingent of draftees within thirty days after a mobilization, and for having at least 100,-000 in training within sixty days. Under present circumstances, it would take 110 days for the first inductee to set foot on a training base. Faced with this evidence last autumn [1979], Congress voted down a move to reinstate draft registration 259 to 155. The rhetoric on the House floor was right out of a 1970 antiwar rally. The reality of our national mood, demonstrated in an April 1979 Gallup poll that showed 76 percent of Americans nationwide and 73 percent of those in the eligible age group favored draft registration, was ignored.

The situation with the reserves is equally bleak. Individual Ready Reserves, those who are still serving out a commitment and thus are eligible to be mobilized even though they do not train with a unit, are 500,000 men short of the number considered necessary to fill the lag between mobilization and the preparation of inductees for duty. The organized reserve, which is designed to feed actual units into a theater of operations within days after mobilization, is 200,000 men short, and is a laughingstock that does not even take itself seriously. It cannot recruit: the Army Reserve is at less than half of its wartime manpower level. Defense politicians have responded by lowering reserve manpower goals to match the number of recruits they believe can be signed up. For instance, the Army claimed in 1978 that it recruited 92.5 percent of its reserve goal, although this was only 48.4 percent of wartime requirements. Nor can the reserves retain: 60 percent quit before they fulfill one tour of duty.

The Carter Administration has been on notice regarding these deficiencies for some time. Its response has been to classify part of the problem and ignore the rest of it. In late 1978, for instance, the DOD ran a paper mobilization exercise known as "Nifty Nugget," which theorized a major commitment of U.S. forces to Europe to help NATO fight a conventional war against Warsaw Pact forces. In light of the overwhelming conventional superiority Eastern European forces enjoy, and the increasing adventurism of the Soviet Union, as well as our own possible hesitation to initiate an all-out nuclear war with Russia in response to a conventional attack on our strategic "periphery," this is not an unlikely scenario. The results, in manpower terms alone, were devastating. As one Army planner put it, "Don't buy any Victory bonds."

Ninety days into such an engagement—twenty days before this country could even deliver a draftee to his training facility—our military would be more than one million personnel short. In some critical combat skills, we would have only 30 percent of the trained manpower needed to fight a war. We would have less than 40 percent of the doctors needed, less than 25 percent of the nurses, and less than half the enlisted medics, thus ensuring that many thousands would die for lack of care. It is impossible to measure what would happen to our aviation forces; aviators require more than a year of intense training before becoming combat-ready.

Confronted with this evidence, Army Secretary Clifford Alexander refused to discuss it, even with members of Congress in closed session. This led Congressman Robin Beard of Tennessee, a former marine and a leading proponent of military preparedness, to claim that "this is a flagrant abuse of the system and does not serve the national interest. The manner in which this information has been handled is nothing short of a national defense scandal."

There are not many members of Congress with the insight and concern of Robin Beard these days. The failure to address defense manpower issues over the past decade shows the priorities of a Congress whose members have an increasingly large lack of military experience, and whose view of the political world was shaped by the gyrations of a vocal minority during the Vietnam protest years. Of the twenty-nine members of Congress born in 1944 or later, only five have served with the active military forces, and only one is an actual combat veteran.

The volunteer Army is an unmitigated disaster. Those who discovered, after fifteen years of calculated silence, that the Vietnam draft fell disproportionately on the poor and minorities, now remain mute before the hard evidence that the cure is infinitely worse than the disease. If present enlistment trends continue, the Army will be 42 percent black by the early 1980s. White enlistees have less education than black, evidence of their socioeconomic status. More than 60 percent of enlistees are from the bottom two categories of intelligence testing. It is so hard to re-enlist a soldier that the Army is now permitting those who fail their skills qualification test to re-up, thus assuring the youth of America that, if mobilization should occur, their NCO's will be unqualified to train them, much less to function themselves. This situation is getting worse every year: in 1979, the intelligence levels of recruits and those re-enlisting were the worst since the volunteer Army began.

Because American males have been conditioned since Vietnam to view the avoidance of military service as honorable and just, and because President Carter's Administration has misguidedly viewed the role of women in the military as an issue more of equal opportunity than of effective national defense, increasing percentages of women are being brought into the service. It is expected that by 1984, 12 percent of the Army will be female, up from 2 percent in 1972. Army Secretary Alexander, a former chairman of the Equal Employment Opportunity Commission, views reluctance to use women in the military through the same prism he did the resistance to blacks in the 1960s: as a product of unfounded bigotry. Using the "narrowest definition of combat that was practicable," he has opened up all but twenty-four of the 305 military specialties to women, ensuring that female soldiers will be directly involved in any future military confrontation. The glowing press releases put out by the DOD about how well this is working may be fooling portions of the American public, but they are hardly deluding the Soviets. Furthermore, our international military credibility is damaged by the reality that no President wants to be the first to send large numbers of American women out to die.

The issue is more than the cultural bias which sometimes held blacks back: it is biological as well. We are the only country in the world whose political process is pushing women toward the battlefield. Contrary to popular mythology, Israeli women do not serve in combat units but rather perform administrative and technical functions that free the men to fight. When three Israeli women soldiers were killed in the 1973 Yom Kippur War, it shocked the nation. The Soviet military, which used women out of necessity in the latter stages of World War II, now has only 10,000 women in a military force of some 4.5 million. If the Soviet World War II experience had been beneficial, it seems logical that they would have capitalized on it.

But quite obviously, the disadvantages of using women far outweigh the advantages. Training regimens in our own military have been watered down. Sexual attractions dissipate a unit's sense of mission, and affect combat readiness in other ways: in 1978, fully 15 percent of the women on active duty in the Army became pregnant. Double standards in performance and discipline have unavoidably evolved; despite what some would like to think, men and women are fundamentally different, and treat each other accordingly. And the product, after all of this confusion, is a soldier who is 55 percent as strong, has 67 percent of the endurance, and has much greater privacy needs than her male counterpart. But how can a male policymaker who debunked the whole notion of military service when he was called upon to serve now invoke the essential masculinity and rigorous nature of that which he avoided?

Because there is no draft, volunteer Army soldiers are wheedled and cajoled by recuiters. This sort of seduction, which has become necessary in the face of recruiting shortfalls that have increased every year, creates an attitude in both the enlistee and the military itself which is destructive to discipline and the traditional notions of service. Enlistees often expect magical, exotic things to happen to them once they "join the people who joined the Army." What they do not expect, and will not abide, is the sort of harsh, demanding regimen necessary to produce disciplined and effective soldiers. And—a recent innovation, compliments of volunteer Army recruiting difficulties—if they don't like the treatment they are receiving, they can simply quit. Under the Trainee Discharge Program and the Expeditious Discharge Program, a person on active duty can leave the service at any time up to three years after his or her enlistment, with a discharge under honorable conditions.

The military, which traditionally has caused many an errant youth to develop self-discipline and motivation, is now discharging people by the thousands at their request, for lack of those same qualities. According to current Army regulations, members who have demonstrated that they "cannot or will not meet acceptable standards" can be discharged owing to "poor attitude, lack of motivation, lack of self-discipline," and "inability to adapt socially or emotionally." The characteristics that help "identify" these soldiers include such formerly resolvable tendencies as being a "quitter," having "hostility toward the Army," having an "inability to accept instructions or directions," and a "lack of cooperation." Since this program was introduced in 1976, more than 190,000 servicemen and women have simply walked away, with discharges under honorable conditions—enough to populate the entire Marine Corps at full strength.

Under this and other such rubrics as motivational problems, character or behavior disorder, inaptitude and unsuitability, fully 40 percent of the enlistees in today's military fail to complete their period of obligation, and yet manage overwhelmingly to receive discharges under honorable conditions. How can a military commander create a properly disciplined environment when his members can simply walk away and still be rewarded for "honest and faithful service"?

The Carter Administration has responded quite creatively to such statistics. Assistant Secretary of Defense John White testified in the Senate in May 1978 that the decline in absences without leave, courts-martial, and nonjudicial punishments showed that "a strong case can be made that our active forces are stronger and better manned than at any time in our history."

Quite apart from the fact that, at the very moment Secretary White was uttering those words, General Brown's combat-effectiveness study was showing that one out of every four tank gunners in the Army cannot even aim a battle sight, the Secretary's statement was circuitous. The decline in the use of the disciplinary process does not indicate that our troops are more disciplined; rather, it indicates that there is not even enough discipline to utilize the process. When a disaffected soldier can simply quit and walk away, with a discharge under honorable conditions, he hardly needs to go over the hill.

Not that people have stopped going over the hill: in 1979, 113,650 servicemen and women did so. Greater than 11 percent of the enlisted personnel in the Navy and 12 percent in the Marine Corps were absent without leave or in a desertion status for some part of that year.

During my last year in the Marine Corps, I briefed a case for the secretary of the Navy involving a marine who had received a bad conduct discharge in 1932 and was asking for an upgraded discharge. The marine, a combat veteran of World War I who had had fourteen years' good service, had been awarded this punitive discharge, the equivalent of a criminal conviction in a civil court, for being AWOL for five days. This seemed extreme to me in 1972, although I certainly viewed his absence as a punishable offense. During my time in the Marine Corps, unauthorized absence did not become grave enough to warrant discharge until perhaps a month, when an absentee became a "deserter" for purposes of identifying his offense. An absentee was most likely court-martialed; a deserter, although rarely convicted of the offense of desertion, was usually thrown out with a less than honorable discharge.

In the volunteer Army, however, a deserter is seldom even court-martialed. As an example of the deterioration regarding this peculiarly military yet important offense, from 1974 through 1977 the military reported 608,000 AWOLs exceeding twenty-four hours. The Army court-martialed almost none of them. In fact, only 11 percent of the most serious offenders, the thirty-day "deserters," were court-martialed. And of these 608,000 offenders, only 2,335 were discharged for the offense. As a referent from another era, more than 29,000 servicemen were convicted by court-martial for being AWOL in 1952 alone.

The cohesion and morale of an army are often measured by its desertion rate and what its leaders do about it. Condoning unauthorized absence destroys the notion of duty and commitment in a military unit, and affects discipline as few other breaches of military custom can. The military becomes simply a job. Soldiers become employees, who show up whenever and in whatever condition they choose. But how does a system stop this when it must beg its members to join, and when those who become annoyed with their service can quit?

A draft would remedy this and other shortfalls, not merely by offering up more manpower and a less delicate command environment, as opponents of the draft so often maintain, but by causing a much-needed reorientation of priorities. The military is not a job, any more than paying taxes is a job. In fact, military service might be equated to a tax. We each surrender a portion of our income to the common good, and we should all be willing to give a portion of our lives in order to assure that our freedoms will not disappear. It is so very basic, and yet so much maligned in the cynical wake of Vietnam: conscription is not slavery, it is societal duty.

Reinstituting the draft would help in yet another, more elemental and equitable way. We created a military, just as we created a society, for ideological rather than mercenary reasons. Detractors of the draft who claim that our natural state, through history, has been draft-free fail to recognize that our position in the world until well into this century was less than preeminent. Nor do they recognize the post-World War II strategic realities. It is fundamentally wrong—and cowardly—in a democratic society to claim that those who stand between us and a potential enemy should be risking their lives merely because they are "following the marketplace," and the military is their "best deal." The result of such logic is today's volunteer Army, a collection of men and women who have been economically conscripted to do society's dirty work, as surely as if there were the most inequitable draft imaginable.

The draft would not make us a nation of militarists; it never has. It would instead leaven the military and at the same time weave those in uniform back into the fabric of our nation. People who work together and depend on each other end up liking each other; that was the great lesson of World

War II, which brought together 16 million American men from all walks of life. The obverse is true of Vietnam, which over a longer period saw 9 million men in uniform, less than a third of the draft-eligible males in the pool, selected out largely on the basis of education or lack of it.

Those who oppose the renewal of the draft claim that the young will refuse to serve, invoking some misconception from the Vietnam days about widespread draft resistance. My bet is that they are wrong, just as they are wrong to invoke Vietnam as precedent. The lesson of the Vietnam draft is not that people will not go if called: only 13,580 men refused the draft during that entire era, while millions went. The real lesson is that a draft, once invoked, should be fair in its application, and should not allow the travesties of avoidance within the law that draft counselors perpetrated during Vietnam. How is a system equitable when Joe Namath, a fabulous athlete, and Tom Downey, now a vigorous, basketball-playing congressman, are found physically unfit for service? In America, only one in three was drafted. In Israel today, 95 percent of the males serve in one capacity or another. There are plenty of desks to sit behind in the Army, in order to free those more physically able to fight. It only remains for a system to refine itself in order to determine who should type and who should fight.

It has become clear that, if we mobilize without a draft, the only men in this country capable of plugging up the dike until replacements can be trained are those who served and fought in Vietnam. DOD mobilization plans presently provide for this contingency, as well as for recalling military retirees. Those who claim that another Pearl Harbor would obviate the need for a draft, and that the time period for mobilization would thus be much shorter than now planned, overlook the reality that the draft had been in effect for a full year before Pearl Harbor, and that fully two thirds of our servicemen in the Great Patriotic War were draftees.

So it would be left largely to the Vietnam veterans to do it again. The group that went once to the well and came away labeled as "suckers" by 63 percent of the respondents in a re-

cent Harris survey would be required, simply because they
did their patriotic duty once, to do it again, while the two
thirds of their age group that stayed home and started their
careers and bitched about the war could do that again.

This is a manifestly unfair possibility, although I have no
doubt that many Vietnam veterans would voluntarily re-enlist if we were to mobilize. And perhaps, come to think of it,
putting Vietnam veterans back into uniform for a while
would be enlightening to today's military. For all the malign-
ing of their Vietnam service, there can be no doubt that they
could aim tanks and fix ships and show up for work.

But our greatest need is to get beyond those old jealousies
from Vietnam, to make our military once again a fighting
force rather than a social lab, and to stop being afraid to ask
the men of Harvard to stand alongside the men of Harlem,
same uniform, same obligations, same country.

---

## IT'S TIME TO BITE THE BULLET ON THE DRAFT[4]

...When the volunteer force was established, one assumption of its architects was that if you attracted people
into the military with good pay and bonuses, and added an
elaborate system of bonuses and other incentives to induce
them to reenlist, they would remain for a career. For a variety
of reasons, this has not happened. One is that White House
and congressional budgeteers have nickeled-and-dimed the
service people on a whole array of cherished benefits—travel
expenses, medical and educational benefits, housing allowances, and the like. This has become an emotional and dis-
heartening subject among military people.

The volunteer army from the start was front-loaded on
pay. Most of the pay raises went to the first-term enlistees,
along with bonuses to persuade them to stay for a second

⁴ Excerpted from article by Juan Cameron. *Fortune.* 101:52–6. Ap. 7, '80. Reprinted
from the April 7 issue of FORTUNE Magazine by special permission. Copyright © 1980
Time Inc.

hitch. Over the past seven years, the pay of careerists has increased by only 70 percent, while the wages of first-term enlistees have risen by 400 percent. At the same time, military pay increases have been significantly below the inflation rate. Since the early 1970's, there has been nearly a 20 percent real decline in pay.

As a result, none of the services today is retaining more than 60 percent of its second-termers, despite cash reenlistment bonuses that can range from $2,000 to $15,000. It is not hard to see why so many are leaving. A Safeway checkout clerk in California makes $300 a month more than a Navy chief petty officer with eleven years' duty. Add in long tours of sea duty, a reduction of benefits supposed to offset the pay differential with civilians, and the result is a Navy that is 20,-000 petty officers short of requirements.

The most skilled military people—computer operators, electronic technicians, doctors, pilots, nuclear engineers—are those that are hardest to retain. A pilot who may have cost as much as $1 million to train presents a serious problem for both the Air Force and the Navy. One with the rank of captain in the Air Force, for example, may earn, with flight pay and allowances, $24,000 a year. But after two years with a commercial airline, he can expect to earn $30,000 and, if all goes well, eventually as much as $90,000. Major General William Usher, the Air Force's director of personnel plans, says that in the mid-1970's his service lost about 400 pilots a year to the airlines. Last year, it lost 3,000 of its 24,000 fliers. Over the next five years, he predicts that the airlines will also need some 80,000 mechanics. To get them, they will be looking to the Air Force and Navy—where the mechanics earn only half the $12 hourly wage paid in private industry.

The utilities are another competitor for trained people. Especially after the Three Mile Island accident, they are expected to step up their raids on naval nuclear personnel. Recently, an official of the Nuclear Regulatory Commission enraged the Navy by advising utilities they should expect to pay $50,000 a year for a good naval nuclear engineer. In the face of such enticements, less than half the Navy's nuclear officers are staying after their five years of obligatory service, despite the promise of $15,000 bonuses.

## The changing mix

While the loss of skilled manpower may be the services' most pressing problem, the changing mix of personnel within the services poses scarcely less difficult dilemmas and stresses. To fill their ranks, for example, the services have turned increasingly to women volunteers, whose numbers have increased to 150,000 today—from 43,000 in 1973. By mid-decade, it is estimated that this figure will reach 250,000. Important and valuable as their services are, they constitute a force ineligible for combat duty.

At the same time, the percentage of minorities—largely blacks and Hispanics—in the services has increased dramatically. They now make up 41 percent of the Army's ranks and 26 percent of the Marine Corps. The military has provided a prime job market for blacks, of course, at a time when their unemployment rate has been very high. By contrast, the white middle class has been shunning military life. Since minorities make up an increasing proportion of the eighteen-to-twenty-six age group, this trend toward a disproportionately large number of black soldiers can be expected to continue through this decade.

The large number of blacks in the military raises social as well as political issues. There are more than a few analysts of the subject who report that the growing number of blacks is affecting the willingness of whites to join up. Some fear the result to be what they call "an Army with the best of the blacks and the worst of the whites." Noting the heavy concentration of blacks in combat units, one Marine general warns that, in wartime, blacks will take a disproportionate number of casualties. As a result, he predicts that this would lead inevitably, as it did during Vietnam, to charges of genocide by black leaders.

Meanwhile, military life is gravely troubled by racial tensions and disciplinary problems with minorities. One Army

instructor in jungle training in the Panama Canal Zone com-
plained to an *Army Times Magazine* reporter: "You can't discipline the blacks because they yell racism. And the officers
are scared of being called racist, so they won't back you up."
The failure to discipline blacks, the instructor added, means
that white soldiers can't be disciplined either: "That's where
we are. It's no discipline for anybody."

Another common complaint that comes from many sergeants and petty officers is that the volunteer recruits are increasingly difficult to train because of their poor educational
preparation and low technical capacity. Until this year, the
Pentagon has maintained that, even though it was getting
fewer people in the top category, it was also getting fewer in
the lowest category (an I.Q. as low as 80). The figures showed
an impressive gain in the middle ground—the so-called Category III.

In the mid-1970's, however, the Defense Department had
changed its testing procedures. Intentionally or not, this
skewed the results upward. A recent sampling indicated that
one-quarter to one-half of recruits who were thought to be in
Category III really belong in Category IV—that is, the group
with less than average mental ability. One senior personnel
officer says his data show 35 percent of the Army volunteers
and 20 percent of the Marines to be of low capability. Defense officials are still studying this sampling. But it may help
explain the dismaying dropout rate of first-term recruits,
which now stands at 30 percent.

From all these difficulties confronting the Pentagon on
military power, there emerge a few inescapable conclusions.
The need to revive registration—including classification—of
men to meet the long-shot chance of mobilization seems
clear-cut and urgent. A standby system of registration was assumed to be essential by those who advocated the all-volunteer service. President Ford's decision to let the system lapse
was based on budgetary reasons, the Vietnam backlash, and
the absence of any serious foreign threat that required it to be
continued. The events of the past year have made it plain that
the decision was wrong.

*Test of resolve*

Only a draft can solve many of the manpower problems now facing the military. It can assure that the services get their needed share of a declining pool of young men during this decade. It would help raise the quality of the enlisted personnel. A very important corollary benefit also would follow from encouraging volunteers, anxious to stay out of the draft, to enter the Army reserves—probably enough of them to meet the immediate manpower needs after any sudden outbreak of ground war in Europe.

Yet even the draft will not remedy what is perhaps the most serious manpower problem—the steady loss of the services' skilled people. There is no blinking the fact that the cure for this is money, lots of it. Senator Nunn thinks it might cost as much as $5 billion a year. Former Secretary of Defense Melvin Laird puts the bill for pay increases to hold skilled men at $10 billion for the first year alone. Obviously, sums of this size raise political problems nearly as sensitive as the draft itself—particularly in a period when the whole federal budget is under pressure.

It seems no less obvious that a readiness to face these problems realistically looms as a test of U.S. resolve—and credibility—before the world generally and our allies particularly. To most of these allies, the obligation of military service has long been accepted as a just burden of citizenship. And the U.S. cannot long continue to do less—while exhorting other free nations to do more—in the common cause of a vigilant guarding of the peace.

## ABOUT-FACE ON THE DRAFT[5]

Over the last year [1979] we have been treated to a series of academic conferences, articles and seminars dealing with

[5] Reprinted from magazine article by Richard A. Gabriel, a faculty member at St. Anselm's College, Manchester, N.H. *America.* 142:95–7. F. 9, '80. Copyright © 1980 by *America* magazine. Reprinted by permission.

the problems of the all-volunteer army. What these discussions all have had in common is their failure to analyze the problem of military manpower from any perspective other than the economic one. The fundamental premises that gave rise to the elimination of conscription and the consequent reliance upon volunteerism to fill the military manpower requirements of the United States have gone unexamined. The debate surrounding the draft has never focused upon the real issue: whether the All-Volunteer Force (A.V.F.) has worked and whether there may be good reasons for a return to conscription.

Even a cursory examination of the facts of the A.V.F. leads one to conclude that a return to the draft is both a practical necessity and a moral imperative. If America is to remain faithful to its social values and its military commitments, it can no longer rely upon the "forces of the marketplace" to meet its military manpower requirements. To do so conceals two devastating truths: The A.V.F. is among the most discriminatory social institutions allowed to exist in the United States since slavery; from the perspective of military power, the A.V.F. is simply not an effective fighting force.

*Social Composition.* An examination of the social composition of the A.V.F. reveals it to be one of the most unrepresentative social institutions in American history. Ironically, during the Vietnam War, opposition to the draft was based on the inaccurate perception that blacks and other minorities were bearing an unfair share of the burden of military service and combat death. The A.V.F. was supposed to put an end to such discrimination and produce an armed force roughly proportionate in social composition to the society as a whole. What has resulted, however, is a military institution that is further removed from representing American society than it has ever been in our history.

The social composition of the A.V.F. today indicates just how unrepresentative and how removed from the mainstream of American society it is. Thirty-six percent of the soldiers in the A.V.F. are black. If Pentagon projections hold, by 1985 fully 65 percent of the army will be black. Blacks are overrepresented in the armed forces by a number three times as large as their proportion in the population. In combat units, an even higher percentage of blacks is found; in some instances, it exceeds 50 percent. While blacks comprise three times their fair share of soldiers in the enlisted ranks, they comprise only half, six percent, of their fair share of officer ranks.

While reliable data about the percentage of other minorities serving in the A.V.F. are hard to come by, at least one prominent sociologist, Charles Moskos, has suggested that over 40 percent of the A.V.F. is being drawn from minority groups. From the perspective of racial and ethnic minority representation, the A.V.F. draws disproportionately more from these groups than from any others. If the A.V.F. is ever forced to do battle, blacks and members of other minority groups can be expected to bear a far greater share of the burden of death than they would normally suffer under a draft.

Another aspect of the A.V.F. is that it is drawn disproportionately from the lower segments of American society, when those segments are defined in terms of educational and economic skills. The percentage of soldiers in what the military classifies as "Category 3B," soldiers that are marginal in their mental capacities, has risen from 10 percent during the Vietnam War to an amazing 59 percent today. Over half of American soldiers are considered by Army testing standards to be mentally marginal, indicating that they are being drawn from the ranks of the educationally disadvantaged. Equally enlightening is the fact that the number of soldiers who have some college experience has dropped dramatically since the end of conscription. Less than 3 percent of the men in the A.V.F. enlisted ranks have some college education at a time when four of every nine students in American society go to college. This is a clear indicator of the degree to which the educationally disadvantaged are drawn into military service under the A.V.F.

Finally, at a point in American history when 83 percent of American youth obtain a high school diploma, only 42 percent of the soldiers in the A.V.F. have obtained one. The drop in educational and learning levels among A.V.F. soldiers becomes graphically evident when the reading levels of American soldiers are examined. In 1973, prior to the end of conscription, the average American soldier read at the 11th-grade level, or about the equivalent of a high school graduate. Today the reading level of the average soldier in the A.V.F. has dropped to the 5th-grade level.

The A.V.F. is really an army of America's poor, its minorities, its blacks and of its educationally disadvantaged. It comprises those in America who have been cumulatively disadvantaged, those who are unable to function successfully within a society and economy that is increasingly complex and requires sophisticated skills. Unable to make their own way in that society, these individuals seek the most available outlet. They enlist in the military service. There is no doubt at all that the A.V.F., since it draws disproportionately from the lower elements of American society, is not representative of that society in any significant way.

Viewed in this light, the A.V.F. is not a truly volunteer army. In point of fact, a form of conscription is already operating; it is conscription by poverty, by lack of opportunity and by disadvantage.

*Fighting Ability.* That the A.V.F. is not representative of American society may be a condition that Americans can live with. But no free society can live long with a military force that is neither reliable nor effective. The A.V.F. simply does not measure up well when examined empirically according to traditional norms of military effectiveness.

Drug use, for example, appears to be pandemic in American units. While drug use is down somewhat from the 30-percent use prevailing during the Vietnam War, at least 28 percent of American soldiers today admit to using drugs regularly. As much as 50 percent of the troops report using drugs for recreational use, and, in a recent survey, 20 percent report using hashish at least five times a week, while 4 percent confess to using hard drugs (heroin and angel dust) at least as frequently. In addition to drug use, one-quarter of all combat soldiers under 21 are problem drinkers and fully 9.5 percent are alcoholics.

Desertion and AWOL rates are another indication of low

discipline levels in American units. Both are higher than they were in the base year 1964 (pre-Vietnam), although they are down somewhat from the Vietnam War years. Last year, however, the Navy had the highest desertion and AWOL rate in its history, while desertion leveled off at roughly 18 per 1,000 in the Army. By any standard, the AWOL rate is up about 60 percent. Once again, these figures indicate the state of discipline in the armed forces.

Fully one-third of all soldiers entering the A.V.F. ultimately fail to complete their first enlistment, because they are found unfit by the military and discharged early. Most have committed some type of disciplinary offense. Low levels of discipline are not only a consequence of the quality of the average A.V.F. soldier, but also of the policy of "managing disciplinary rates," namely, the practice of dealing administratively with problems that in pre-A.V.F. days would have been dealt with by court martial or judicial punishment. Although the A.V.F. has lowered standards for both entrance into and remaining in service, in 1979 the Army still had the lowest rate of honorable discharges in its history. So low had disciplinary standards fallen that a soldier charged with a drug offense could still expect to receive an honorable discharge 93 percent of the time; a soldier charged with desertion could expect a 96-percent chance of receiving an honorable discharge.

The raw-recruit material available since the end of the draft has proved very difficult to train. The Army admits that its M.O.S. (military occupational specialty) shortfall is 42 percent, indicating that at least that percentage of soldiers are filling military jobs for which they are not adequately trained. In the recently completed Army Readiness Study, it was found that of a maximum performance score of eight points, the average combat soldier was able to perform his military skill at a level of only 1.8. Twenty-nine percent of tank gunners tested, moreover, could not correctly aim their guns. The number of soldiers unable to perform their most fundamental military missions has increased rapidly in other areas. Meanwhile, as the availability of top-quality soldiers is on the decrease, the intelligence requirements to operate and maintain ever more sophisticated equipment have dramatically increased.

But there is probably no more crucial indicator of the A.V.F.'s weakness than the psychological preparedness of the troops to engage in combat if forced to fight. A study of the Berlin Brigade, generally considered one of our elite combat units, showed that 53 percent of the soldiers admitted that they did not trust their officers or N.C.O.'s and would not be prepared to follow them in combat.

*Why the A.V.F.?* Why is it, then, that a social institution that has failed on both normative and empirical grounds, on both ethical and pragmatic lines, continues to exist when all indications seem to require that it be abandoned and conscription reinstituted?

In order to grasp the attraction of the A.V.F., especially to today's draft-age population, it must be understood that the end of conscription in 1973 was not a military decision. The record shows that the military opposed the decision to abandon conscription precisely on the grounds that it would result in a poor quality army that was highly unrepresentative of American society. The decision to replace conscription with an all-volunteer armed force was made by President Nixon in a deliberate effort to pacify the campuses and their opposition to the Vietnam War by removing the threat of military service from the nation's politically powerful middle class and its college-educated elites. The creation of the A.V.F. was a political decision that did not proceed from any pragmatic assessment of America's military manpower needs or of its social values.

What I have called elsewhere the "tyranny of the economists" also significantly influenced the introduction of the A.V.F. Since 1960 and the appointment of Robert McNamara as Secretary of Defense, the United States has excessively relied upon economic models and managerial values in the area of military decision making. The difficulty with economic models as guides to decision making, however, is that they tend to be one-dimensional; the measurable financial cost becomes the most important criterion in arriving at decisions. Economic models, moreover, define man as one-dimensional, as a calculating being who assesses losses and gains in terms of whatever option is most "economic." Besides being overly simplistic, such models are blind to the larger social questions and to the question of social values. In most instances, they are devoid of ethical considerations.

The economic model, moreover, has been wrong more often than right. The four basic assumptions of the Gates Commission, which recommended the A.V.F. in 1973, have all proved false. That commission assumed: 1) that there would be an adequate supply of available manpower from which to draw a military force; 2) that the quality of that manpower would be adequate for military skills; 3) that attrition rates for those joining the A.V.F. would drop; and 4) that the retention of those in military service would increase. Events have proven all these assumptions wrong. In spite of the reduced size of the armed forces, the A.V.F. has not been able to recruit enough men (or women) to fill its quotas; every year the shortfall grows. Attrition rates are the highest in recent history and, as a corollary, retention rates are among the lowest.

*Conscription as a Solution.* Military service is not just another economic choice, nor is it solely an individual obligation. It is a community obligation, special in nature and imposed in the name of the community on the principle that membership in the community implies a willingness to defend it. This link between the rights of the individual and his obligations has always been one of the greatest strengths of democracy. In the matter of military service, moreover, it not only involves risking one's own life but it also implies a certain responsibility for the lives of others in the community.

Under such conditions, it is clear that the determination of who does and who does not enter military service cannot be allowed to rest on purely economic calculations. To so regulate military service undermines a fundamental value of American democracy: that all men count equally before the community. As a social institution, the volunteer system in practice imposes the burden of possible death on an increasingly narrow segment of American society—on its poor, its minorities, its ill-educated and its disadvantaged. In practice, it marks a return to the "social worth" doctrine of earlier times, when it was possible for privileged members of the community either to escape military service altogether or to hire substitutes. To continue it can only cause serious rifts in the social fabric. There must be a better way.

It is sometimes argued that any system of conscription would allow some people to escape military service, and that is most certainly true. But the question is not one of finding a perfect system as much as finding one that shares the burden as equitably as possible. It seems obvious that if the United States were to return to a system of conscription in which all physically, mentally and morally fit individuals were assigned a number and selected by lot with no deferments, the simple law of large numbers could ensure the maximum possible equality before the law. A statistically representative cross section of the American people would be drawn into the military, so that the military would closely represent the society that it serves and for which it may well be asked to die. This would spread the burden of risk, hardship and death throughout all social classes and educational levels rather than concentrating it on the narrow segment of the country's poor.

If military effectiveness, moreover, is at least partially a consequence of the quality of the raw material that the military must train, then the selection of a military force on the basis of a relatively fair conscription system cannot help but result in better-quality soldiers, thus producing a more effective fighting force. It would certainly produce a force without much of the drug, discipline and training problems that are commonplace in today's A.V.F. Such a system admittedly would not be perfectly representative, nor would it reduce in every instance the chance of an unfair burden of service. But it would most certainly reduce it to levels far below those experienced under the present system.

The debate as to whether or not the United States ought to return to conscription is no mere academic exercise, for it involves serious pragmatic and ethical questions. In times of conflict, whatever system we choose decides who lives and dies. If we continue to draw so disproportionately upon our poor for those who will bear the burden of military service, we reveal a glaring contradiction in American values. A society that espouses egalitarianism and equal protection of the law can hardly make exceptions when dealing with questions of life and death. Democratic values and habits cannot long endure when the ultimate risk of membership in any society, in this case death on the battlefield in its defense, is not shared equally or at least near-equally. A return to conscription would therefore seem to be an ethical and pragmatic necessity, if the United States is to remain faithful to its social ideals.

The truth of the matter is that since 1973, the system has been rigged to exempt precisely the middle and upper classes of American society from military service. These classes did not serve or die in Vietnam, and they have not served since Vietnam. The A.V.F. continues their privileged exclusion from the obligation only to impose it on the economically and socially less fortunate.

A return to the draft will not be easy, for the A.V.F. serves very well the interests of the upper and middle classes, which are politically powerful and capable of making their influence felt. It may therefore be doubtful whether the draft, no matter how fair, can be reinstituted at the present time. On the other hand, we should be under no illusions concerning the cost in democratic values if we fail to change the present system. Despite the obstacles, our path is clear: A return to the draft is necessary, if America is to remain both militarily strong and ethically consistent to the values that have made this Republic what it is.

## IV. AGAINST A MILITARY DRAFT

## EDITOR'S INTRODUCTION

Opposition to a draft developed almost immediately across the political spectrum following President Carter's request for draft registration. Religious groups, antiwar activists, pacifists, coalitions of women and of students, the American Civil Liberties Union as well as conservatives, such as economist Milton Friedman and political columnist James J. Kilpatrick, all voiced their opposition. On the national political front President Reagan (while still a candidate), Republican Senator Mark O. Hatfield and Democratic Senator Edward M. Kennedy expressed opposition to compulsory military service, particularly in peacetime. Senator Hatfield stated: "This nation was founded to serve the people, not vice versa . . . A coercive, mandatory service to the state is one basis of totalitarianism."

President Reagan in his commencement address to the graduates of the United States Military Academy at West Point in May 1981 expressed a traditional viewpoint: ". . . our country has a unique tradition among the nations. Unlike the other powers with armies of conscripts, our military was always composed of citizen volunteers. In times past, the standing army was a skeleton force that expanded in wartime to absorb the draftees, the conscripts . . . We had always believed that only in the most severe national emergency did a government have a claim to mandatory service of its younger citizens. . . ."

In an editorial in *Saturday Review,* Norman Cousins contends that in the nuclear age "A large standing army no longer has meaning in terms of national defense . . . We seem less governed by reality than by the obsession to imitate the

Russians. Is there no escape from the macho madness that is disfiguring American society?"

The executive director of President Nixon's Commission on an All-Volunteer Armed Force thinks the issue of a draft never would have been raised if military salaries had been increased over the last few years. William H. Meckling, a strong supporter of the volunteer force, in an interview with *Fortune* thinks "The real question is whether the people who are responsible—and by that I mean the Congress—are doing their job right. If they want a better force, they can always get it simply by raising the pay."

Gordon C. Zahn, a conscientious objector during World War II and a member of Pax Christi U.S.A., perceives "a growing trend toward militarization" in this country and proceeds to present the pacifist viewpoint in the next article from *America.* In the wake of Iran and Afghanistan and the resumption of draft registration he sees young Americans being reduced "to the status of mere symbols, pawns to be used in a shadow game of international power politics . . . with the sudden expansion of one nation's military forces . . . the net result is that the likelihood of war increases. . . ."

In the next article, Milton Friedman, economist and contributing editor to *Newsweek,* declares ". . . a draft is not desirable. It is a divisive measure completely in conflict with the basic values of a free society."

"A continued attempt to militarize the American conscience" is how peacetime draft registration is described in the concluding article by Joseph A. Tetlow, associate editor of *America* who strongly urges President Reagan to cancel it promptly. "If we must have this quasi-fourth branch of government [the military], then it should be what it is at present, all volunteer."

## THE GAMES NATIONS PLAY[1]

. . .The argument in favor of restoring the draft, inevitably enough, is that the Russians have at least two million men in uniform and that this disparity is likely to expose the United States to grave dangers. No one says anything about the fact that the vast bulk of the Soviet forces is stationed along the 5,000-mile border the USSR shares with the People's Republic of China.

It will be said, of course, that the Russians won't take our foreign-policy declarations seriously if they see little evidence of our ability and will to fight. This was the argument used to justify the home bomb-shelter program in the early Sixties. It was and is the argument used to justify the building of missiles and super missiles. It was and is the argument used to justify the stockpiling of nuclear explosives that can obliterate every city on earth and make the planet uninhabitable. One would suppose that presiding over a switchboard of total annihilation would relieve us of any feelings of inadequacy. But no; we seem less governed by reality than by the obsession to imitate the Russians.

Is there no escape from the macho madness that is disfiguring American society? When are we going to discover that our true strength and security depend not just on weapons but on our ability to make our society work? When are we going to attach at least as much importance to productivity, creativity, and the imaginative uses of freedom as we do to balance-of-power strategies? When are we going to see the relationship between spending 150 billion military dollars annually and the disastrous conditions of inflation? When are we going to stop supporting three separate military establishments—an army, a navy, and an air force, each with its own heavy overlapping in ordnance, personnel, and intelligence services?

[1] Excerpted from editorial by Norman Cousins, editor. *Saturday Review*. 6:8. S. 15 '79.

We became entrapped in Vietnam because of the same kind of thinking that is behind the current attempt to restore the draft. At every point along the way, we allowed ourselves to be led along by specious arguments. We convinced ourselves that our most important mission as a nation was to demonstrate our muscle rather than to conform to our history. After the French left Indochina, we were told that the entire area was in danger of being solidified under a unified communist banner—and that we could head off this grim eventuality simply by sending a little military aid. Then we were told that a few American officers were needed to instruct the local people in the utilization of such aid. Finally, we were told that the rest of Asia would pay no attention to our policy unless we committed American divisions. Then came the quicksand and the endless graves.

History has proved the government's statements to the American people about the Vietnam War to be both incompetent and absurd. We were told that the Vietnamese were puppets of China, but today the "puppets" and the "puppeteer" are engaged in fierce recriminations and border fighting. We were told that the communization of Indochina would create a unified ideological force that would march in solid formation against the rest of Asia; but the Communist nations of Indochina are now warring among themselves. We were told that China and Russia would team up against the West. But the main threat of nuclear war today comes from the unresolved tensions between these two nations.

And now the same people who gave us all these boomerang situations want to activate a peacetime military draft that runs counter to our traditions and that, only a decade ago, divided this country beyond anything experienced since the War Between the States. The single most important thing we should have learned from the Sixties is that we do not put men and women in uniform unless they have a cause that is tied to a clearly understood moral purpose that is generally connected to the American future and that is directed to the making of a safer world. We should have learned from our experience that Americans are not poker chips to be used in the international game of posturing and blustering designed to maintain a balance of power. The Bismarckian concept of fending and thrusting may have had its place in a Europe where history was an endless chain reaction of plot and counterplot, but in an age in which nations are only a push-button away from a mutual cataclysm, game-playing becomes little more than a fuse for igniting continental destruction.

A large standing army no longer has meaning in terms of national defense. Ballistic missiles, MX launchers, submarines with thermonuclear warhead delivery systems, all these will bypass the defending army and strike at the real target—the life of the nation itself.

The government cannot have it both ways. It cannot ask for billions of dollars for inflicting instant death on an enemy in a war that may last a few minutes, and then turn around and ask for money to support a 19th-century form of warfare. National security in a nuclear age depends on an unremitting effort to create a durable peace through world order. If we haven't yet learned that fact, the largest army in the world will not save us.

## THE DRAFT IS AN UNFAIR TAX ON UNLUCKY YOUNG MEN[2]

Q. FORTUNE, members of Congress, and military leaders have said that in terms of numbers and quality the volunteer force is inadequate to meet a national emergency. What's your assessment?

A. It's working about as well as the commission staff predicted it would when we made the study in 1969. The real question is whether the people who are responsible—and by that I mean the Congress—are doing their job right. If they

[2]Reprint of interview with William H. Meckling, dean of the University of Rochester Graduate School of Management and executive director of President Nixon's Commission on an All-Volunteer Armed Force. *Fortune.* 102:169–170. Jl. 14, '80. Reprinted from the July 14 issue of FORTUNE Magazine by special permission. Copyright © 1980 Time Inc.

want a better force, they can always get it simply by raising the pay.

In the past three or four years, wages of enlisted personnel, particularly the first-termers, have declined some 15% relative to civilian employees in the same age group. If you have that kind of decline in any field, you'd expect that fewer people would want to go into it.

*Q. Scores on the aptitude tests given to enlistees appear to be going down, and only 58% of the new recruits are high-school graduates. Isn't the military getting to the bottom of society's barrel in order to meet its recruiting goals?*

A. We could have an armed force of Ph.D.'s if we were willing to pay for one. But if Congress continues to do nothing about compensation, I think we're going to see a further deterioration.

*Q. Critics charge that there is less discipline in the volunteer force, and that it is becoming a military of minorities.*

A. It is certainly true that there is less discipline in the military now than there was under conscription. The commission predicted that would happen. You can't impose as much discipline on a man who has volunteered and can resign fairly easily. The issue, however, is how well volunteers will fight. It is not clear that coercion and petty standards in small things—haircuts, for example—produce a more effective fighting force.

The commission also predicted an increase in the number of black soldiers in the all-volunteer Army, but we were talking about something on the order of 19%—not the 37% or so that we now have. Presumably the military is offering better jobs to many young blacks than they can get in civilian life. If the Pentagon says we have to reduce the numbers of blacks, what it's really proposing is that we deprive the blacks of those opportunities. I think we ought to look at that proposition very carefully.

*Q. Are you advocating an across-the-board pay increase of 15%? I estimate that would cost at least $5 billion.*

A. If they put me in charge of military compensation I could find most of the money in the present budget. First,

I would modify the traditional compensation structure that gives military men of the same rank the same base pay whether they're nuclear-submarine technicians or combat soldiers or clerks. We have volunteer truck drivers, clerks, and bakers coming out of our ears. In other areas—like combat and the technical fields—the military cannot get enough of the right kind of people. What I would like to see is some transfer of pay from the clerks, cooks, and truck drivers to the people in combat or technical specialties.

I would also reduce that huge component of military pay that is retirement compensation. We should abolish the existing plan completely for the newcomers and replace it with one in which vesting begins at the first reenlistment. To have people retire after only 20 years at half pay—and that amount is constantly being adjusted upwards as active-duty pay rises—is something we can no longer afford.

A big part of the compensation problem is the way Congress manages it—very badly. There is no reason why Congress couldn't give each service a budget and let them decide how to pay people.

*Q. Are the big reenlistment bonuses working?*

A. Obviously not, or we wouldn't have all these problems. In terms of management, it's a bad idea to give people huge sums of money in advance of seeing what they actually do. Instead, why not spread that compensation out over a period of time in terms of pay raises a soldier gets for performing well.

*Q. But a conscripted force would be a lot cheaper, wouldn't it?*

A. The real costs of the military are the things we give up in order to have a defense establishment. If I take someone out of the civilian economy and put him in the military, the cost is what that person would have produced as a civilian.

There isn't any doubt whatever that a conscript force costs *more* than volunteers. If the military takes a volunteer, it's drawing from that part of the supply curve of people for whom being in the military is a most attractive occupation. That costs society little. Conscription takes people from all along the supply curve—some people way at the top. The costs to society are high when physicists are put to work washing the decks of ships.

Q. *But physicists could be put to work in the Navy as physicists.*

A. Yes, but if they are conscripted and not paid as physicists they are being asked to pay a very high tax. The issue is really not costs. It's who's going to pay those costs. When you have a conscript force, instead of taxing the general public to get the right kind of people to volunteer, you are levying a high tax on the very small subset of the population that you draft.

In our study we estimated that draftees and draft-induced volunteers gave up $2 billion in forgone earnings in 1967—an average tax rate of 48% of their wages in civilian life. Adding in personal income tax, their effective tax rate was 51%. The average income tax paid by their counterparts who were not drafted was only 10%.

There's no way in the world that we'd ever agree to a tax system that imposes such a huge tax on a group of 300,000 men a year who happen to turn 18 years old, and happen to be qualified to serve in the armed forces. But we do this in the disguised form of conscription.

I get in trouble with some of my friends who say, "What's wrong with these young people today who don't volunteer, who don't feel any responsibility to serve their country?" I say, "I don't understand these old people who don't feel any responsibility for paying for their country's defense."

Q. *So in spite of your recommendations to transfer existing military funds, you're saying that an improved military force would cost more money.*

A. Like any civilian business, if you want higher-quality people, you've got to pay more. We can always end up with the right numbers, even with the population of 18-year-olds declining. As an economist, though, it seems to me that the military should adapt to this demographic fact by slightly reducing the size of the military force. Economics suggests that in the face of a declining youth population, we ought to substitute more capital—weapons—for labor.

*Q. But another ground war in Europe would be labor-intensive. In a simulated European war that the Pentagon played on computers—an exercise called Nifty Nugget—there weren't enough people to sustain the initial period of the conflict, and reserves couldn't be rounded up in time to make a difference.*

A. I find the Nifty Nugget exercise a case of analytical fraud. Let me point out one thing. We've almost never used the reserves as replacements. During the Vietnam war we kept people enlisting in the reserves by never calling them up. Why bother with a reserve that you're never going to use, like the Nebraska Navy?

The second problem: if you're talking about reserves with quick reaction capability, those forces have to be in existence, trained, equipped, and ready to go. Once you start computing the costs, it comes to a very large fraction of maintaining an active duty unit. Faced with this fact, Congress has always chosen to put the money into the active force.

*Q. The commission that you headed came out in favor of a standby draft. Do you support draft registration?*

A. I was opposed to registration then, and I'm opposed now. We didn't have conscription when we went into World War I. Congress authorized it on May 18, 1917, and by June 5, nearly ten million people were registered. That's not now, that's 62 years ago, before computers.

Actually, if the military needs the names of 18-years-olds, the government could just as easily get them from the Social Security records. Special legislation would be necessary to have the Social Security Administration run a tape for the head of the Selective Service.

*Q. Do you consider the all-volunteer force only a peacetime one, or can it work in time of war?*

A. Under conscription, the government tells people that they have to go off and serve—that is, it threatens them with jail if they don't go. That comes down to pure, unadulterated physical coercion, which I object to on freedom grounds.

I also object to all the arbitrary ways of deciding who will go and who will not—including the lottery. What if Congress decided we should pay our taxes on a lottery basis? Those who lose will pay as much as five times the average in taxes. That's the kind of inequitable lottery conscription is.

During World War II, there was a lot of waste because of conscription. Far too many people were put in the military and not enough were left at home producing. So I think that even in wartime conscription is probably a bad idea.

---

## THE ALREADY DANGEROUS WAR MENTALITY[3]

Now that President Carter has had his way and Selective Service is once again registering young Americans, the pressure will be mounting for the obvious next step, full-scale resumption of peacetime conscription. Generals who once voiced their opposition have suddenly become converted to the failings of a volunteer army and the seductiveness of the draft. Coupled with the President's more recent desire to increase his authority over the nation's reserve forces, these developments testify to a growing trend toward militarization that confirms the warnings issued over the past few years by our leading peace organizations. In January, for example, Pax Christi U.S.A. opposed the registration proposal as but one more element of what it described as a "momentum building up in our country for violent retaliation" for the frustrations caused by Iran and Afghanistan. Serious as those issues are as violations of human rights and international integrity, Pax Christi felt it necessary to remind American Catholics in particular that this momentum also endangers peace.

In the intervening months the disposition to contemplate the possibility of military responses to foreign policy setbacks or anticipated threats to oil supplies has grown more pronounced. Bishop Thomas Gumbleton's words have lost none of their validity: "The nation and the world are caught in a

---

[3] Reprint of magazine article, The Draft: An Occasion of Sin?, by Gordon C. Zahn, a member of the Executive Council of Pax Christi U.S.A. and a professor of sociology at the University of Massachusetts—Boston. *America.* 143:46–9. Ag. 2–9, '80. Copyright © 1980 by *America* magazine. Reprinted by permission.

rapidly escalating crisis which could, if not halted, lead to war. Already government leaders and ordinary citizens are speaking of war as an imminent, perhaps inevitable, response to the international problems we face. The rhetoric of threat and reprisal has come to dominate diplomatic discourse at precisely the time when Pope John Paul II continues to voice his urgent pleas for peace and disarmament."

Christians, and especially Catholics, must consider what we and our church can and must do to stop, or at least slow, the accelerating drift toward a war that is forbidden. To this point our record has been mixed at best. The U.S. Catholic bishops—still the official spokesmen for the Catholic community—have taken what appears to be a public stand critical of registration and conscription, but, as is all too often the case, the thrust of what they say has been blunted by the quibbling reservations that are so much a part of episcopal pronouncements. And, as is almost always the case, there has been no noticeable effort to follow through with effective, practical action to achieve the goals they proclaim.

The February 1980 statement issued by the Administrative Board of the U.S. Catholic Conference provides a classic illustration of both failings. Accepting in principle the Government's right to call for registration, the bishops went on to declare that the exercise of this right required "convincing reasons for this at any particular time." One might have expected some evaluation of just how "convincing" Mr. Carter's reasons at the present time were, but such was not forthcoming. The only explanation advanced by the Administration, apart from the claim of efficiency, which was disputed by the Selective Service's own reports, was that the President intended to "send a message" of his (and, presumably, the nation's) displeasure over the Soviet aggression in Afghanistan. This is hardly adequate justification for an action designed to disrupt the lives of a whole generation of young men (and women, too, if President Carter had had his way).

If, as Christians, we reject the instrumental use of human beings, some question should have been raised about reducing these particular human beings to the status of mere symbols, pawns to be used in a shadow game of international power politics. Though we have the President's pious assurances that he has no intention of reinstituting the draft, it would be unwise to place too much confidence in them. The registration build-up will contribute to the already dangerous war mentality, and the mere availability of large numbers of potential draftees is almost certain to open the way toward an even more "adventurous" foreign policy of confrontation and threat.

The February statement by the U.S. Catholic Bishops was more definite in restating the Church's traditional opposition to conscription and national service and in proclaiming the legitimacy of conscientious objection as an option for Catholics. More should be required here as well. If, as many of us believe, a return to peacetime conscription will follow once the election is out of the way, this careful expression of ecclesiastical opposition will have to be supplemented by the same kind of concentrated and organized lobbying efforts that have been so much in evidence in the abortion issue. There may be some comfort in the fact that other major Presidential candidates (Reagan, Kennedy, Anderson) have taken a position against the draft; unfortunately there is little in their political commitments or past records to assure that any one of them would be able, or would wish, to withstand the pressure that is certain to build once the military leadership is convinced a return to the draft is within its grasp. In this respect the Senate debate—in its tone as well as in its predictable outcome—might be taken as the advance shadow of coming events.

Two of the familiar arguments against peacetime conscription have already been mentioned in passing. The interference with the freedom of choice of the individuals who will be subject to a draft becomes all the more unjust when that interference comes at a time when they are preparing for their future careers. (That this interference is justified in purely "symbolic" terms merely adds one more dimension to the injustice.) The second objection is the danger that the virtually unlimited availability of large numbers of men trained in the military arts provides the temptation and the opportunity for policymakers to take positions and make demands which, under other circumstances, might have been more marked by prudence and restraint. Even where this does not occur, the sudden expansion of one nation's military forces is likely to incite prospective rivals to respond in equally provocative fashion. The net result is that the likelihood of war increases as the already diminished stock of mutual trust (John XXIII's only sure foundation of lasting peace in the nuclear age) disappears completely.

There are other equally telling objections to conscription, especially in time of peace, but I should like to bring attention to one that is all too often ignored. Since it focuses more directly on the effects it may have upon the moral and spiritual dimensions of human behavior, it should be of primary concern to the Christian. Stated most bluntly, a military draft should be opposed because it is, to introduce a sadly outmoded term, an occasion of sin. At first glance the reader might be tempted to shrug this off as an exercise of rhetorical excess on the part of one whose pacifist bias is fairly well known. Upon reflection, however, one might discover that the application of that term is really not so inappropriate after all.

Certainly I would not suggest that the military life is sinful in itself or that everyone associated with it is, by that fact alone, excluded from the state of grace. The issue is rather one of personal disposition and the probable impact of exposure to military values and discipline at an age when the individuals exposed are most vulnerable to their appeal.

An occasion of sin, as moral counselors once described it, was any situation or setting in which one put himself (or allowed himself to be put) where the likelihood of sinful behavior was heightened because the capacity to recognize or resist temptation was diminished. It is in the latter sense that submitting to a military draft (and, since it makes such a draft more likely, registration) fits the definition. The term fits in other respects as well, of course. For one thing, preparing young Catholics to use the patently unjust weapons of modern war—and I would include much of our "conventional" arsenal as well as nuclear weapons in that category—should be every bit as objectionable to our moral sensitivities as would be a required course in the techniques of abortion for pre-med students. Nor can we overlook the celebrated temptations to "sins of the flesh" traditionally associated with barracks life, a concern which has led many military chaplains to see their moral guidance responsibilities almost exclusively in terms of combatting fornication, other sexual aberrations, cursing, drinking, gambling and the like.

I have no objection to placing these moral dangers high on the list of dangers to individual sanctity, though it is probably safe to assume that the normal patterns of adolescent experience in contemporary America have already exposed the average 18-year-old to most of them. I would agree that these temptations are probably intensified by barracks life and peer pressures. As such, they are rightfully a matter of serious concern to parents and others interested in preserving or restoring traditional Christian behavioral values in an increasingly secularized world.

Nevertheless, it would be a serious mistake to see them as the only or even the most compelling reasons for regarding the imposition of required military service as an occasion of sin. That is to be found instead in the intended effects and purposes of the training program itself. We begin with a consideration which should be perfectly obvious: It is the rare 18-year-old who has achieved the degree of spiritual and intellectual maturity needed for making the "heavy" moral decisions military service forces upon him. Does this war in which he is called to serve, or this specific military engagement in which he is involved, respect the limits set by his religious beliefs? Is he aware that such limits exist? Is it morally right for him to intentionally injure or even kill this particular "enemy" or, for that matter, any other human being at any time, under any circumstances? How is he to reconcile the Gospel lessons calling for love of enemy, for forgiveness of wrongs, for turning the other cheek, with the drill sergeant's insistence that the prime objective must be to survive in a brutal "it's us or them" contest to the death?

Not only is the average 18-year-old ill-prepared to find the answers; he will probably not be aware that such questions are there to be faced. And it will be the job of those entrusted with his military preparation to see that he not be bothered by such doubts or misgivings lest his morale and that of others around him be weakened. Individual moral judgment on such questions is to be supplanted by patterns of indoctrination and unquestioning obedience to superior authority that leave little inclination or opportunity to consider other options or alternatives. The independent conscience that should be developing to full maturity at this age is stunted and smothered instead.

All this applies to the voluntary recruit as well, of course; but in his case society has not played the decisive part in placing him in the setting and subjecting him to the process that constitutes this particular occasion of sin. The volunteer is there by choice and, to that extent, these risks and temptations are part of the package he bought, however unwisely. The draftee is twice victimized. In this sense it is something of a scandal to find responsible leaders playing such prominent roles in a conspiracy to force millions of young men into a situation of moral jeopardy. It is even more a scandal that they can do so confident they will encounter nothing worse than half-hearted opposition from the caretakers of public morality. Not even that. Usually the response will be one of reluctant approval and support. All too often, enthusiasm.

In fairness, though, one must grant that, judged by its record of the past, the Catholic hierarchy deserves a measure of commendation for being only *half*-hearted in its acceptance of registration and open in its opposition (still, alas, in a half-hearted and contingent mode) to peacetime conscription and national service. Even greater credit is earned by its recognition of conscientious objection as a legitimate option for young Catholics and its repeated calls for legal provision for selective conscientious objection. These are significant advances over the far less generous attitudes that prevailed as recently as World War II. As my history of the only professedly "Catholic" camp for objectors to that immensely popular war (*Another Part of the War: The Camp Simon*

*Story*) makes clear, the few who took that stand then—and I was one of their number—received little respect and even less support from the American Catholic community, bishops included.

The February statement is to be welcomed as a giant step toward the "entirely new attitude" called for by Vatican II. Interestingly enough, though it stops far short of using my "occasion of sin" formulation, it shows the bishops share my general concern in at least two respects. What Thomas Shannon has described as "the principle of selective obedience" (*Render Unto God*) finds expression in the declaration that "the state's decision to use force should always be morally scrutinized by citizens asked to support the decision *or to participate in war.*" This means it is no longer only a refusal to serve which must be justified; now the decision to accept service is to be subjected to the same requirements of moral deliberation and justification.

This, obviously, brings us back to the problem I have raised. Will the citizen taken in his youth and subjected to military indoctrination *ever* be fully capable of conducting the kind of scrutiny the bishops recommend? The statement addresses the problem in its concluding sentences:

"We also affirm that the decision to enter military service and subsequent decisions in the line of military duty involve moral questions of great importance. Hence, the issues of registration and conscription raise questions of the kind and quality of moral education that takes place in our educational system. Specifically, it raises the question of what educational and counseling resources are available to a person facing registration or conscription. In adopting this statement of public policy on registration and conscription we call upon schools and religious educators to include systematic formation of conscience on questions of war and peace in their curricula and we pledge the assistance of appropriate diocesan agencies in counseling any of those who face questions of military draft."

Unfortunately, what is left unasked and unexplored is whether even this is enough, whether it will be possible for the teen-age boy to maintain the correct conscience formed through such education and counseling once he is exposed to military indoctrination and discipline. My own answer to the question, then, is no. To the extent that the military training program succeeds, all future judgments concerning issues of war and peace are likely to be affected.

Statements of moral principle, welcome and even necessary, are never enough in themselves. What has been lacking thus far is clear evidence of a concerted episcopal commitment to action and, equally important in this particular instance, a driving sense of urgency. Other issues—liberalized abortion, school aid, etc.—provide striking evidence of what can be done; there is no reason for not displaying the same commitment to action with regard to registration and the draft. Even though the struggle has been lost on registration, it is still possible to marshal effective opposition to peacetime conscription. If this is not done, a second and more disastrous defeat is certain.

This is not simply a matter of directing the church's efforts toward political leaders and legislators, however. A more energetic follow-through is needed to awaken the Catholic faithful to the issue and its implications as well. It is all too evident that the February statement has had virtually no impact upon the religious community in whose name it was issued. Most Catholics are quite unaware of its content, or indeed, of its existence. If nothing else, the Administrative Board should make some effort to discover and assess the extent to which individual dioceses have acted to correct the deficiencies recognized in that document. Are peace studies programs being incorporated as required subjects in Catholic schools and Confraternity of Christian Doctrine programs? What has been accomplished to provide the counseling and support services that have been pledged?

If, as I suspect, there are dioceses in which the laudable principles of the February statement have not been put into actual effect, one might look to the U.S.C.C. to encourage and assist them in taking the necessary steps. It is already months too late for such beginnings, but every effort should be made to have such programs in full operation before the end of the year. It will not be easy. As a member of Boston's archdiocesan Justice and Peace Commission, I know how difficult it is for even so "advanced" a diocese to meet the test. As things now stand, the first batch of registrants are already being denied the assistance and guidance they need and to which they should be entitled. Even worse, in far too many of our dioceses they are being caught up in the registration procedure without the comfort of knowing their spiritual leaders are at all interested enough in providing such resources.

Indications are that even greater problems lie ahead. We are told that Selective Service, anticipating a great upsurge in applications for conscientious objector status, has recommended restricting eligibility to practicing members of religious communities that forbid participation in military service. Though this would be a flagrant act of discrimination against Catholics and other denominations whose teaching includes the traditional distinction between "just" and "unjust" wars, no public protest has been heard. The hierarchy is on record with its repeated recommendations that the conscription law be revised to recognize such selective conscientious objection, but little effective lobbying has been done. This makes it a simple matter for legislators and other Government officials to ignore those recommendations. Here, too, so little has been done to promote this particular cause that most Catholics are unaware that the suggestion has been made.

A determined effort is being made by such groups as Pax Christi U.S.A. and the Catholic Peace Fellowship to meet the needs of the young people now subject to registration and the draft, but their resources are too limited to do all that must be done. Moreover, lacking official status they are usually written off (by the Government and, all too often, by their fellow Catholics as well) as extremist peacemongers of questionable orthodoxy. There is no escaping the fact: Only the bishops, acting in concert and within their separate dioceses, can hope to accomplish the goals to which they have been pledged. It is time they begin.

Registration and the draft are not the only issues relating

to questions of war and peace. The arms race, so explicitly condemned by the Holy See, continues and expands. Papal appeals to abandon the ways of violence because they are not in accord with the Gospel and, therefore, cannot be Christian (Paul VI) and because they can never be the way to justice (John Paul II) have had little noticeable effect upon the course of international events. What gives registration and conscription claim to priority for American Catholics is the immediacy of the issue: It is being decided now and in the next few months. Of perhaps greater importance are the longer range consequences of failure here; for once we are reconciled to a program that systematically turns our young people over to the state for military indoctrination and experience, we will have reduced their capacity to choose the course that might give them success where past generations have failed.

Actually, there is more at stake than that. "To reach peace, teach peace," we have been told. The opposite, I am afraid, is equally true. If we sit quietly by while our young men (and women) are compelled to "study" war and undergo preparation to use weapons and strategies that are clearly immoral, we shall have placed them in an occasion of sin and opened the way to the war which, by Thomas Merton's memorable assessment, would be a crime "second only to the Crucifixion."

---

## A DRAFT IS NOT DESIRABLE[4]

---

Draft registration is neither necessary nor desirable. It is being proposed to reassure the public at home, not to frighten the Russians. It is not necessary, because our military weakness derives neither from a shortage of manpower nor an inability to increase the number of people under arms by voluntary means. It derives from a failure to build new

[4] Reprint of magazine article, "Draft Registration," by Milton Friedman, 1976 winner of Nobel prize in economics and contributing editor, *Newsweek*. 95:79. F. 11, '80. Copyright © 1980, by Newsweek, Inc. All Rights Reserved. Reprinted by Permission.

weapons—one after another canceled by President Carter. Recruitment difficulties with the all-volunteer force reflect primarily the erosion of the inflation-adjusted compensation of first-term enlistees, relative both to their civilian counterparts and longer-service personnel. When the draft was replaced by an all-volunteer force in 1973, the pay scales were adjusted appropriately. Since then, Congress and the Administration have not seen fit to maintain the pay scale for first-termers. If it is desired to increase the size of the armed forces, either in general or for specialized personnel, that can and should be done without a draft.

*Bad Arithmetic:* It is said that we cannot afford to do so. That is nonsense. Proponents of a draft point out that total personnel costs of the armed forces are more than 50 per cent of total military spending. However, only about 11 per cent of that goes for the pay of first-termers—in 1979, total personnel costs were $58.4 billion but only $6.3 billion of that went to pay people serving fewer than four years. Even a major increase in the pay offered new recruits would involve only a minor increase in the total defense budget. The rest of the total personnel costs is for the pay of longer-term personnel, officers, civilians, and retirement benefits. And only first-termers would be recruited by a draft.

Registration would have a minor effect on the time involved in getting manpower and womanpower if a draft were reinstituted. The time-consuming steps are not registration but selection and training. That was demonstrated in earlier drafts. And even a full-scale draft would not provide personnel rapidly enough for a modern war. That must be fought largely by forces in being.

Draft registration is not desirable because a draft is not desirable. It is a divisive measure completely in conflict with the basic values of a free society. Every emergency has shown that in time of real need there is no shortage of patriotic citizens eager to defend the country. Draft registration simply diverts attention from the real source of our military weakness.

That source is the welfare state. In 1970, spending on defense was 40 per cent of the Federal budget, and 8 per cent of GNP—one and a half times the budget of HEW. In 1979, spending on defense was 23 per cent of the budget and 5 per cent of GNP. The budget of HEW was one and a half times the defense budget. These developments have occurred under Republican and Democratic administrations alike. Carter has simply continued on a well-worn path.

*The Real Culprit:* Transfer expenditures have absorbed taxable capacity that had supported defense—and much more as well. We cannot undertake a major rebuilding of the military without cutting down the drain that the rest of the budget imposes on the taxpayer—whether directly through explicit taxes or indirectly through inflation and borrowing. There is, after all, a limit to the total taxable capacity of the economy. Look at Britain's decline as a world power, which, as C. Northcote Parkinson somewhere points out, owes much more to the growth of the welfare state than to any other single factor.

No series of symbolic acts, no expressions of bellicose intent will change that brute fact. If we try to follow a policy of guns plus welfare-state transfers, I fear we shall end up with neither.

President Carter has acknowledged the drastic recent change in his opinions about Russia—a courageous admission of almost unbelievable prior naïveté.

Is it outside the bounds of possibility that he could acknowledge that past fiscal and military mistakes have made it impossible for us to respond effectively to Russian aggression now or in the immediate future, but that we are going to change course in light of the present danger?

It is time that we desisted from purely symbolic acts designed to reassure the American public and garner votes in November rather than to frighten the Russians. We must do the unthinkable—cut the burden on the economy that comes from picking all of our right pockets to fill all of our left pockets and instead embark on a crash program to strengthen our defenses.

## PRESIDENT REAGAN AND THE DRAFT[5]

During the Presidential campaign, Governor Ronald Reagan opposed peacetime registration for the draft.

His opposition had diminished by the time he fielded a question at his first press conference on Jan. 30. He apparently still felt, as he had during the campaign, "that the advance registration . . . would not materially speed up the process if an emergency required the draft." But he claimed that his nine days in office had been spent in the Cabinet room macerating the budget, "and so I just have to tell you that we will . . . make a decision on what to do with it down the road some place."

That "some place" ought to come soon. One of President Reagan's first executive orders ought to cancel the advance registration of young males.

It is not that the registration has failed. Opponents like the Rev. Barry Lynn of the Committee Against Registration for the Draft predicted that 20 or 25 percent of the 3.8 million eligible men would not sign up. But spokesmen for the Selective Service announced in December that 87 percent had registered on time and 6 percent, late. By January, probably 95 percent had filled out the card.

Furthermore, the nationwide brouhaha threatened for last July and August fizzled, and the second round—those born in 1962 registered during the second week of January—went on with little notice. All told, the peacetime registration probably could be called at least a technical success.

Nonetheless, President Reagan ought to cancel it for five good reasons.

First, the registration is not what President Carter called it in January 1980, "necessary for rapid mobilization." His own Defense Secretary, Harold Brown, had denied that a few

[5] Reprint of magazine article "President Reagan and Registration for the Draft," by Joseph A. Tetlow, associate editor, *America.* 144:139–40. F. 21, '81. © America Press, 1981.

months earlier. A review of military manpower and of the Selective Service System, Mr. Brown had testified to the Senate Armed Services Committee, "does not lead to the conclusion that peacetime registration is necessary."

Just one week before President Carter's call, his Director of the Selective Service System, Bernard D. Rostker, argued the same thesis. He reported that peacetime registration would save a militarily insignificant amount of time and cause resentment; the "option chosen" by the Service was to leave registration until after a draft was legislated.

Mr. Rostker also noted that peacetime registration would cost too much, which is the second reason why an economy-minded President ought to call it off. The bill, passed by the Senate on June 12 and by the House on June 26, authorized spending $13.3 million to set up the registration, which Mr. Rostker estimates will cost $23.8 million a year to keep up. That seems a small sum next to the defense outlay of $184.4 billion for 1982, but it is as much a waste of money as the "consultants' fees" President Reagan has just pared. Its aim is swift mobilization, but it registers the wrong people for that.

Here is the third reason to end the registration. In any national emergency, Senator Charles McC. Mathias Jr. (R., Md.) argued last February in an attempt to amend the Senate bill, the services will need skilled personnel—computer experts, rocket mechanics, pilots—not untrained recruits. There are hundreds of thousands of men and women who are "skilled, able and ready to move in, and move in promptly," Senator William Proxmire (D., Wisc.) pointed out, because they have already been trained in the all-volunteer services. Where are they? The Selective Service System does not know. No one does. But they are the people a peacetime registration should identify and keep track of; they are the ones the nation would need in an emergency requiring swift mobilization.

The fourth reason for canceling peacetime registration of 18-year-old males emerges from the history of the draft. During the War of Revolution, only Virginia and Massachusetts tried a draft. George Washington's letters show the draftees' attitude toward it: When they felt like it, they went home.

During the Civil War, the draft caused the worst riots the nation has known. On July 13, 1863, for instance, rioting in New York City erupted that in four days gutted stores, burned mansions, killed hundreds and was quelled only when troops poured in to stop it. In spite of four separate draft calls, only a very small part of the Union Army was directly drafted.

Two subsequent conscriptions, however, worked well. The draft that began in 1917 supplied two-thirds of the nearly four million men who fought World War I. The draft that ran from 1940 to 1949 worked just as effectively for World War II.

Very briefly after that war, the armed services were composed completely of volunteers, but the Korean War launched a very much less popular and less equitable draft in 1952. It continued through several transmogrifications until the winding down of the Vietnam War. The last call-ups were in December 1972, although registration continued until 1976.

The Vietnam War wrecked the draft. These are the entries in a dictionary of American history: *Draft cards, burning of, 1965; Draft deferments, 1967; Draft evasion, 1968.* During the last years, 40 percent of those eligible applied for Conscientious Objector status and about half of them received it, as the status was vaguely and pragmatically redefined. Even so, when the Treaty of Paris was signed on Jan. 27, 1973, more than 60,000 Americans had fled the draft to Canada and Europe; 200,000 had failed to register and been referred to the Justice Department for prosecution as felons; another quarter of a million had failed to register but were not prosecuted.

The bitterness and confusion have by no means worn away entirely. An astonishing number of secular, denominational, ecumenical and interfaith groups swiftly organized between January and July 1980 to counsel conscientious objectors. Many denominations followed the Society of Friends and the Lutherans in taking some official stand on conscientious objection, and 36 religious leaders, including five Catholic bishops, denounced the peacetime registration as "a continued attempt to militarize the American conscience."

That charge may or may not be true, and, if it is true, the attempt may or may not succeed, but if the present poorly enforced registration continues, it is more likely to aggravate the American conscience and build up the resentments that Mr. Rostker predicted. What reaction does American history suggest to the next draft: willing, like the reactions to the drafts of 1917 and 1940? Or rather recalcitrant, like those to the drafts of the War of Rebellion and the Civil War? It depends a good deal on how any future conflict begins, of course, and on how clear and compelling the cause of the United States is. But it also depends on a clear national perception that the draft is not only necessary but also equitable. The peacetime registration is likely to cloud those perceptions.

And this raises the final reason why Mr. Reagan ought to cancel the peacetime registration. It is souring the country's attitudes not only toward the draft, but toward government itself. Probably a quarter of a million have refused or neglected to register. They are thereby felons, liable to five years in prison and a $10,000 fine. Not one of them has been prosecuted. In fact, the Selective Service does not even know who they are.

Furthermore, half of those who ought to be eligible in some sense, American women, have been deliberately cut out of the registration by Congressional action. A great number of them will not be mollified, and the American Civil Liberties Union has taken its case against the constitutionality of an all-male registration to the Supreme Court.

In a sense, this peacetime registration does not show the "national will" Mr. Carter said it would show. It shows the Government's willingness to enact a law which is inequitable and feckless. Such a law should be wiped out.

Contrary to the intense convictions of the Founding Fathers, the country now has a standing army. During more than a generation, it has caused all the problems the Fathers foresaw—huge expense, inequitable burdens, willful bureaucracy among them—even though the reasons against having a standing army have grimly altered.

If we must have this quasi-fourth branch of government, then it should be what it is at present, all volunteer. In that case, the only sane kind of peacetime registration is a clear record of all alumni and alumnae of that volunteer service— and a clear notice that those who have resigned from it will be called to serve in any national emergency, having volunteered themselves in the first place.

President Reagan can accomplish that readily. He has promised to accomplish part of it by canceling peacetime registration of untrained young men. That is one promise he ought to keep promptly.

# V. THE WOMEN'S ISSUE

## EDITOR'S INTRODUCTION

The most controversial part of President Carter's draft registration program was his proposal to register women. A House of Representatives subcommittee, however, struck down this provision of his plan without debate. In Philadelphia though, a three-judge Federal panel ruled the draft registration law unconstitutional precisely because it discriminated against both sexes by barring women and placing the burden only on men.

The women's rights movement faced a frustrating and paradoxical dilemma on whether to endorse registration or not. Many feminists argued that being for the Equal Rights Amendment also meant being for a draft for women, even though large numbers of them had actively protested against the Vietnam war. Some disliked the idea of women being inducted into the male-dominated military and thus opposed even registration. Others felt compelled either to endorse the draft reluctantly or simply to oppose it for both men *and* women on moral/pacifist grounds.

For the anti-ERA forces, the issue was cut-and-dried. From the beginning one of their major arguments against passage of ERA was that women would automatically become subject to the draft. They now waged a campaign not only against ERA, but also against the draft. For them the issue was one and the same.

The first article in this section is a *Newsweek* summary of the varied jobs that women currently hold in the armed forces. "Amid all the controversy, what isn't generally realized is that women have already established a beachhead in the U.S. armed forces. In fact, the U.S. now has more women

135

in service—and a greater percentage of women—than any other country."

The next three articles are examples of how different writers wrestle with the issues of the draft and feminism. Writing in *New Republic*, Lisa Myers contends that "Ultimately, treating men and women equally for purposes of registration is a simple matter of social justice . . . If the feminists fail to put aside their differences and unite on this issue . . . they will have only themselves to blame for legislating and perpetuating inequality."

However, Gloria Steinem, writing in *Ms*, thinks women "could end up *with* the draft—and *without* the Equal Rights Amendment . . . Women share the general suspicion that this peacetime draft is dangerous and unnecessary, for both women and men."

In the next article, Mary Jo Salter, staff editor of *Atlantic*, points out that "President Carter, who would belong to the feminist camp, put his position on the . . . issue craftily: 'Equal responsibilities deserve equal rights.' The responsibilities would come first—in life, as in that sentence." She feels that "The perception of war as natural, even inevitable, is historically a male one . . . women interested in effecting a human liberation might have a piece of history in their hands waiting to be molded. What if they gave a registration and none of us came?"

The concluding article from *U.S. News & World Report* details the major arguments for and against women's draft registration as presented to the Supreme Court. The pro-registration group holds that "There is no legal justification for males-only registration [and] excluding women from registration 'perpetuates . . . ancient sexual stereotypes.' " One argument submitted to the Court against the registration of women is that Congress alone has the power expressly granted by the Constitution to decide military policy. "Here, it is inappropriate for a court 'to substitute its judgment for that of Congress.' "

This argument, in fact, was the basis of the majority opinion when the Supreme Court announced its decision on June

25, 1981. ". . . Perhaps in no other area has the Court accorded Congress greater deference. In rejecting the registration of women, Congress explicitly relied upon its constitutional powers."

Feminist groups were disappointed by the Court ruling and agreed with the minority opinion filed by Associate Justice Byron R. White who stated "I discern no adequate justification for this kind of discrimination between men and women."

## WOMEN IN THE ARMED FORCES[1]

For a man about to shatter 204 years of military tradition, Commander in Chief Jimmy Carter was remarkably nonchalant. He quietly boarded a helicopter for a weekend at Camp David, leaving aides to distribute a written statement announcing his plans to register women as well as men for the draft. "My decision," the President wrote, "is a recognition of the reality that both women and men are working members of our society. It confirms what is already obvious . . . that women are now providing all types of skills in every profession. The military should be no exception."

. . . Carter will send separate his-and-hers proposals to Congress—one asking for $20.5 million to revitalize the Selective Service System to register men; the other asking for the authority to register women. Under Carter's plan, all 19- and 20-year-olds would be required to report to their local post offices—perhaps as early as this summer—to fill out forms stating their names, addresses, birth dates and social-security numbers. Beginning in 1981, all 18-year-olds would be required to do the same. Carter said that his plan was not a move away from the all-volunteer force, simply a time-saving measure to help mobilize troops in case of emergency. And he

---

[1] Excerpted from staff-written magazine article. *Newsweek.* 95:34–42. F. 18, '80.

stressed that he had no intention of sending women into combat.

'Gesture': Even so, the idea of registering women has set off a nationwide debate. It has galvanized both supporters and opponents of the women's rights movement, revived anti-draft protests on college campuses, split the Pentagon and raised fundamental questions about the role of women in American society. Congress, which must amend the current Selective Service laws if women are to be included, is badly divided. The betting on Capitol Hill is that Congress will appropriate the money to register men, but that the question of women will be scuttled in committee. Many congressmen say that registering women will not enhance military preparedness. "If they're not going to be used in combat," says Rep. Richard White, chairman of the House subcommittee on military personnel, "then registration is just a gesture." The American Civil Liberties Union has vowed to challenge the constitutionality of any registration plan that does not include women—and the whole matter may well end up before the Supreme Court.

The public has very mixed feelings about whether to draft women, according to recent polls. And a *Newsweek* poll ... of young people 18 to 24 conducted by the Gallup Organization shows that if the draft is restored, most men say women should be included (61 per cent to 35 per cent), while most young women oppose being drafted (58 per cent to 39 per cent). The respondents did favor registration for all, but 58 per cent said young people would protest or evade the draft if it were called at this time. Should women serve in combat? Two out of three said yes, but only if they volunteered to fight. One out of five said no.

The issue has created a dilemma for feminists. Most generally oppose both registration and the draft for anyone but say that if men are required to register, women should be, too. "We are full citizens. We should serve in every way," says the National Organization for Women's Eleanor Smeal. Feminists charge that the all-volunteer forces would not be short of people if the military did not discriminate against its present female recruits. Many feminists also fear that the draft issue will hurt chances for ratification of the Equal Rights Amendment. Others argue that it would help, on the ground that if women must serve to defend the Constitution, they should be guaranteed equal rights by it. President Carter concurred. "Equal obligations," he said, "deserve equal rights."

Anti-feminists counter that the whole notion of drafting women is the fault of the women's liberation movement—and that had the ERA been passed, Congress would have no choice but to include women. "President Carter has stabbed American womanhood in the back in a cowardly surrender to women's lib," charged Phyllis Schlafly, who says she has already gathered more than 100,000 signatures on petitions to Congress. "We are not going to send our daughters to do a man's job," she vows.

*Beachhead:* Amid all the controversy, what isn't generally realized is that women have already established a beachhead in the U.S. armed forces. In fact, the U.S. now has more women in service—and a greater percentage of women—than any other country. There are 150,000 women in the Army, Navy, Air Force and Marine Corps—about 8 per cent of the total—and the figure will reach 12 per cent by 1985 even without a draft. "Our country cannot afford to ignore the skills and resources women can bring to the military," says retired Adm. Elmo Zumwalt.

The distaff buildup began when the U.S. abandoned the draft in 1973 and set up an all-volunteer military. Pentagon planners eyed demographic statistics showing that the number of eligible men would drop sharply in coming years—by as much as 25 per cent in 1992—and realized they would have to expand the role of women greatly to meet peacetime quotas. As the Defense Department mustered a major drive to recruit women, many traditional barriers to women broke down: they were admitted to the service academies and allowed to take blue-collar jobs, to command coed units, fly noncombat aircraft and serve on noncombat ships. "The use of women is no longer an option, it's a requirement," says Coast Guard Capt. J. P. Randle.

*On Alert:* Today, women can join up for jobs ranging from torpedo repair to military intelligence. At Davis Monthan Air Force Base near Tucson, Ariz., women guard the Titan II intercontinental ballistic missiles. At Fort Campbell, Ky., they teach paratroopers survival skills. At Pease Air Force Base, N.H., they refuel giant C-5 cargo planes 26,000 feet in the air. In the Indian Ocean, near the Persian Gulf, they are on alert aboard the U.S.S. Dixie. At Fort McClellan, Ala., Maj. Gen. Mary Clarke commands 13,000 soldiers—75 per cent of whom are men. And at the U.S. Military Academy at West Point, the first class to include female cadets will receive commissions this spring.

Women are still excluded from any posts in which they are likely to see combat—by law in the Navy, Air Force and Marine Corps and by policy in the Army. That means they are currently shut out of infantry and artillery specialties, duty tours on fighter planes, most Navy and Marine ships and from any Army billets that would put them closer than 15 miles to the front. But the Pentagon has repeatedly asked Congress to rescind those restrictions; failing that, it has narrowed the definition of combat to assign women to as many jobs as possible. "We cannot afford to waste human talent," says Army Secretary Clifford Alexander, who has led the Pentagon's fight for expanded women's roles.

By most accounts, the women have proved remarkably capable. They have placed top in their classes at the Navy, Air Force and Marine officer-candidates schools, qualified for the crack Army sharpshooters team and won places in the prestigious White House honor guard. Because quotas for women are relatively small, recruiters can be choosy— women recruits are generally older, better educated and score higher on aptitude tests than their male counterparts. They drink less, commit fewer drug offenses, go AWOL less often and present fewer discipline problems. Many have surprised battle-tested men with their technical abilities. "I tell my sergeant, 'Get me more like Darlene and Susie, and we'll have a topflight squadron'," says Col. John Paganoni, commander of an aircraft-maintenance section at Pease AFB.

"Women have to do it better," says Staff Sgt. Debbie Hollingsworth. "We can't afford to do just an average job."

*'Crutches':* Still, women are physically not able to perform some tasks as well as men—especially infantry skills. After years of studies, the Pentagon has declared that women have only 55 per cent the muscle strength and 67 per cent the endurance of men. Men have more upper-body strength, and can better withstand temperature extremes, Army tests have found. On average, women are shorter, lighter and slower; many can't maintain the 30-inch regulation Army stride. "It's not a women's problem, it's a size problem," says Molly MaGuire, a sports-medicine expert at Fort Jackson, S.C., the Army's coed basic-training camp. This has presented problems in integrated training. "If we let the platoon march to the average female speed, then we can't meet the requirements," says Fort Jackson Drill Sgt. Donnie Feltman. "If we made the women keep up with the men, we'd have a whole platoon of women on crutches."

Because of the physiological differences, the military has been forced to change some of its standards for women. The Air Force Academy in Colorado Springs, for example, had to allow women one extra minute for the 2-mile run—or risk failing 81 per cent of its female cadets. At West Point, women do flexed arm hangs instead of chin-ups, take karate instead of boxing, and shoulder 8-pound M-16 rifles instead of 11-pound M-14s. At Fort Jackson, women do only eighteen, not 35, push-ups in two minutes, and need not qualify on the rifle range. At Parris Island, S.C., the Marine Corps' boot camp, women are excused altogether from infantry field training and the grueling obstacle courses. They only get to look at a combat marine in full regalia in the classroom, taste his C-rations and pass his helmet around.

*Football:* Many combat veterans say women should be banned from battle for physical reasons. "In Vietnam, when the monsoon hit, our whole valley was under water," adds James Webb, an ex-Marine and author of the combat novel, "Fields of Fire." "We had to get out on ropes with 70 pounds of equipment on our backs. Most women couldn't handle that." Webb and others think that changing standards for women have given them a false sense of physical accomplishment. "You can take football and modify the rules so women can play," he says. "That's fine—until they face the Dallas Cowboys and get slaughtered."

But many military women dismiss such arguments as largely irrelevant. As weaponry and warfare have become more sophisticated, "intellect has replaced brawn," says retired Air Force Gen. Jeanne Holm. Adds Rep. Patricia Schroeder, a member of the House Armed Services Committee: "How much muscle does it take to launch an ICBM?" Today, fewer than 10 per cent of the jobs in the military require actual infantry duty, according to the Pentagon. "How many chin-ups you can do is not going to matter when you're commanding a platoon," says Brig. Gen. Joseph Franklin, commandant of cadets at West Point.

Furthermore, many women point out, they are already hoisting, lugging and hauling about as much weight on stateside tugboats, for example, as they would on a destroyer, and piloting a fighter-bomber requires no more strength than flying a transport or cargo plane. "There are small men in the military who've done just fine," says Sgt. Erlene Thomas, 25, who, as a Marine rescue specialist, is trained to jump out of helicopters and haul in drowning men twice her size.

*Instincts:* The cultural and emotional arguments against women in combat may be harder for women to overcome. "No man with gumption wants a woman to fight his nation's battles," says Gen. William Westmoreland. Sociologists point out that American girls are conditioned against the emotional reactions necessary for battle. "Boys are taught to defend themselves, girls are taught not to fight," says Alvin Green of the Menninger Foundation in Topeka, Kans., who predicts that many more women than men would opt out of the service in wartime. Some military experts fear that the presence of women would interfere with the male camaraderie they say is crucial in warfare, and that the male instinct to protect women might hamper coed combat units.

In addition, opinion polls consistently show that the public is strongly against sending women into combat. Some people worry that if women are captured in combat, they will be sexually abused. Others simply can't stomach the idea of women being killed in war. Says West Point Cadet 1/C Mike Ungar: "It's going to be one hell of a shocker when women are shown on the 6 o'clock news coming home in body bags."

A surprising number of women—both inside the military and out—agree that they do not belong in combat. "I feel a strong commitment to my country and everything," says Roberta Nedry, 19, a student at UCLA. "I just don't see myself in an infantry battalion with a rifle in my hand." Agrees Marine Pvt. Lori Harps, 20: "I think it's a man's place to do the fighting." But many women insist they are willing and able. The possibility of combat "is one of the reasons I came back to the Air Force," says Sgt. Susan King, 23, who recently re-enlisted after her first tour. "We're hurting in this country and somebody's got to take responsibility." "I'm scared of dying, just like anybody else," adds Marine MP Manuela Montoya, 21. "Why should men have to fight for their country if women don't?"

Throughout the services, military women complain that the combat restrictions close off job opportunities to them—even in posts that do not involve combat. Extensive sea or flight experience is required for many promotions, for example. And because of the need to rotate men out of combat-ready posts, there are limits on the numbers of women who can hold even clerical and administrative jobs. "If women take all the shore billets, there will be no place for the men when they come back from the sea," explains Navy Capt. A. C. Eastman. As a result, despite manpower shortages, Navy recruiters are turning away qualified women.

What's more, while nearly 95 per cent of the "MOS's"—military occupational specialties—are open to women, the 5 per cent that are closed represent roughly 21 per cent of the total peacetime jobs. Female cadets at West Point, for example, found that they were shut out of more than half of the usual assignments for second lieutenants because they involved infantry, armor and artillery. And nearly 95 per cent of all slots in the Marine Corps are currently off-limits to women.

*'Second-Class':* Most Pentagon brass agree that the range of jobs for women should be wider. They plan to increase the number of women in the all-volunteer forces from 162,000 to 250,000 (including reserves) by 1985, and they want more flexibility in deploying them. Thus, they have continued to seek relaxed combat restrictions—whether or not they send women into battle. "It isn't so much a big push to use women in combat as it is to understand how women perform in a variety of military jobs," says Assistant Secretary of Defense Robert B. Pirie Jr. "It seems to me intolerable to ask 250,000 women to join the military for a second-class career."

Career opportunities are precisely what attract many young women to the military today. The armed forces have always been a "poor man's college," and women want the same technical training, veteran's benefits and chances for higher education traditionally offered men. Gunnery Sgt. Mattie Hudgins, for example, joined the Marine Corps because she couldn't afford college; now, she has the equivalent of a B.A. in economics and is studying for her law degree. Women say the military also offers them equal pay for equal work and a crack at jobs they could not get on the outside. "There's no way I could have achieved co-pilot status on a commercial airliner at the age of 27," agrees Air Force Capt. Irene Graf, who flies a KC-135 refueling plane. "They're coming in job-minded," grouses Sgt. Maj. Eleanor Judge, a "lifer" who has spent the last 30 years in the Marines. "They're saying, 'The Marine Corps has so much to give me,' instead of 'I have something to give the Marine Corps'."

*Adventure:* And, like soldiers throughout history, women sign on out of sheer boredom and wanderlust. "I was just hanging out at home, partying till 6 and sleeping past noon," explains Frances Mitchell, 18, a new Army recruit. Adds Vicky Zelauskas, 22, a yeoman aboard the U.S.S. Gompers stationed at San Diego Naval Base: "My friends are going to live in Willingboro (N.J.) forever, but I'm going to see the world."

Many women find the service to be mostly work and not much adventure. "I'm ready to go somewhere," says Seaman Shannon Munn, 19, whose first assignment aboard the U.S.S. Gompers was the age-old duty of chippin' and paintin'. "I've been out of port exactly once and all we did was sail around in circles." But the military does offer a degree of authority and responsibility most women never dreamed of in the private sector. "The experience is incredible," says Air Force Second Lt. Nancy Barnett. "I'm in charge of public relations for this whole base. I'm only 23, for God's sake!" Women are also finding that the stereotypes—that they are all lesbians, amazons or whores—are fading. "There are still a lot of officers who let you know they don't think you belong in their Marine Corps," says Lt. Sarah Fry of Camp Pendleton, Calif. Still, all across the country, men are taking orders from women—even if they don't always remember that it's "Yes, Ma'am!"

There have been scattered reports of sexual harassment. At the Fifth Army's base in Frankfurt, West Germany, officials installed bars on the windows of women's barracks after hearing of assaults in the area. Some women say they are afraid to walk through their bases alone at night. And just last week, officials at Fort Meade, Md., launched an investigation into charges that women had been coerced into trading sex for favorable treatment. But in general, military women say the problem is exaggerated. "You have your whistles and your sly, stupid remarks, but after three years in the Navy, you learn to ignore it," says Yeoman Zelauskas. Fort Jackson's commander, Maj. Gen. Lucien Bolduc, set up a hot line for anonymous complaints; in three months, there have only been nine calls—none about sexual harassment.

But fraternization on duty is a problem. In general, the services forbid romances between officers and their subordinates—to preserve discipline—and most branches enforce it strictly. Even among couples of equal rank, there are rules; men, for example, are barred from women's quarters. The Navy has warned sailors on coed ships against any "public displays of affection." (Handholding on the U.S.S. Gompers, for example, can bring a $400 fine.) Nevertheless, dating and sex is common throughout the coed military. "Relationships have interfered with the business of the day," concedes West Point's General Franklin. "But you can't legislate human nature." While some military couples put off marriage until they complete training, others rush to the altar to take advantage of the extra living allowance for married personnel and the chance to move out of the barracks.

*Expecting:* Inevitably, pregnancy has come to the new armed forces—and at an alarmingly high rate. Last year, 14 per cent of the women in the Army became pregnant; about half of them were not married. Over-all, the Pentagon estimates that 8 per cent of U.S. military women are pregnant at any one time. The military has adjusted calmly to the phenomenon. No longer ground for compulsory discharge, pregnancy is a "temporary physical disability," and new mothers are eligible for up to six weeks paid postpartum leave. They can also be released from service immediately, if they choose: "It's one sure-fire way out of the Army," one private explains.

Many military moms choose to stay, however, so the Pentagon had maternity uniforms designed. One plucky marine even completed the strenuous officer-candidate school at Quantico, Va., while six months' pregnant. Pregnancy does cause womanpower problems for the military. According to regulations, mothers-to-be must be evacuated from overseas posts after the eighteenth week, and they are not allowed at sea. Last year, the captain of the U.S.S. Vulcan had to quickly replace two female officers who discovered they were pregnant just hours before the ship set sail for the Mediterranean to join the Sixth Fleet.

Even more troubling to Defense Department officials is the large number of single parents in the military—18,000 in the Army, for example. All single parents must sign a statement that they have lined up a legal guardian for their children if they should be mobilized or killed. Some women stationed overseas have missed maneuvers because they couldn't find baby-sitters, or brought their children along. In a real emergency, some experts fear that soldier-parents will stop to worry more about their children than their duties. "What do we do to assure readiness?" asks author Webb. "Do we turn the Army into a baby-sitting service?"

All these issues will no doubt be aired in Congress in the coming months. Even before Carter's call for registering women, the nation was well on its way to integrating women into the armed forces. If registration is approved and women are ultimately drafted, they will fill many more noncombat roles, freeing men to fight in case of war. But the nation should be under no delusions that this is an egalitarian system. It would be made so only if women take part in combat. The country could choose to move in that direction, but that would mean overcoming centuries of cultural tradition and accepting the very real physical limitations of women. For the time being at least, most Americans seem unwilling to take that ultimate step.

## A GIANT STEP TOWARD EQUALITY?[2]

Eight Bible-packing Pentecostal ministers marched into Senator Nancy Kassebaum's Wichita office determined to save her wayward political soul. It was scripturally sound to reinstitute draft registration, they assured her, citing chapter and verse which prophesied a Soviet takeover of the Middle East. But to include women is anti-God and anti-family, they proclaimed, and would rot the moral fiber of young America. "Phyllis Schlafly must be loving this one," Kassebaum later observed.

Gross exaggeration, distortion, and misrepresentation abound in the initial wave of reaction to President Carter's proposal to register 19- and 20-year-old men and women. The right rails about debasing the flower of womanhood and about women degrading the Army. The far left conjures up

[2] Reprint of magazine article by Lisa Myers, a reporter for the *Washington Star*. *New Republic*. 182:15–9. Mr. 1, '80. Reprinted by permission of THE NEW REPUBLIC. Copyright © 1980, The New Republic, Inc.

visions of the high school football hero and homecoming queen arriving home in unisex body bags from an unjust, far-away war. Young men and women are not being told to pack up their blowdryers and head for the Khyber Pass. They are asked only to walk to the neighborhood post office. The most deadly weapon they have to handle is a Bic pen.

Registration is not the draft, nor necessarily even the harbinger of a return to peacetime conscription. Neither is it the preamble to a declaration of war. It would, however, demonstrate national resolve and willingness to sacrifice to friends as well as foes. The US has been and will be asking Western allies to go along with economic and political reprisals against the Soviet Union—measures that in some cases will entail more sacrifice from them than from us. Registration would be a meaningful symbol that this nation too will sacrifice—a fact subject to international question over the last decade. Registration is a signal to the Kremlin that the trauma of Vietnam has not so damaged the national psyche that the US won't fight back when its interests or allies are threatened.

Although in military terms registration does not improve conventional capabilities, certainly it can be viewed as part of a broader effort to enhance US readiness to respond to a national emergency. If war broke out tomorrow and President Carter ordered immediate and full mobilization, it would take more than a month before the first inductees could be processed. Right now, the Pentagon doesn't even know where to find them. Under the registration proposal, which provides a list of bodies, the first inductions would occur 13 days after mobilization.

Those who oppose registration do so largely on the ground that it is a step toward war, a show of militarism. For some reason, many of these same antiwar activists consider it dishonorable to prepare oneself for a possible conflict. That's for the warmongers, they say. They want Amtrak—to ride in the opposite direction. But it is difficult to find a war in which a country was attacked because of its nonpareil military prowess. Poland wasn't the demonstration project for every European bully since Catherine the Great because it afforded a tough match. "You noticed that the Soviets attacked Afghanistan, not China," notes one administration official.

As for young people themselves—women included—registration should prompt serious reflection of their personal obligation and commitment to country, a process missed by half a generation. "Picking up that registration form is likely to make you think about what kind of commitment you are willing to make and what your priorities are in life," Kassebaum says. "That is a healthy exercise in itself."

Women have been performing military roles successfully since long before they were granted regular military status in the real [men's] army in 1948. In World War II some 20,000 women served in a variety of capacities—as pilots, gunnery instructors, and naval air aviators. They landed on the beaches of Normandy and received Purple Hearts. Women now constitute seven percent of the armed forces and are deemed capable of filling 95 percent of all job categories. Female participation in the military is projected to rise to some 200,000, or 11 percent of all forces, by 1983. Contrary to the assertions of certain conservative lawmakers, women have not contributed to a decline in the overall quality of troops. Pentagon studies indicate that, with the exception of tasks that require considerable upper-body strength, women perform virtually all jobs at least as well as men. In areas requiring dexterity or perceptual skills, women actually outperform their male counterparts. Moreover, women in the armed services "generally are of higher mental aptitude than men," says Robert Stone, acting deputy assistant secretary of defense.

Some legislators object to the encoding of women on grounds that it is likely to bog down implementation of registration at a time when the Kremlin is making menacing sounds. In fact, failure to include women is the primary threat to delay of registration. Men-only registration undoubtedly will be challenged in court as an unconstitutional denial of rights under the Fifth Amendment. The constitutional view held by six of the nine current Supreme Court Justices is that sex-based discrimination is allowable only if certain rather stringent criteria are met. As spelled out in the precedent-setting 1976 case of *Craig v. Boren,* differentiation between sexes is allowed only if it serves "important governmental objectives" rather than merely "old notions" about the roles of men and women in society. Further, the court held that the sex-based classification must be "closely and substantially" related to the accomplishment of those objectives. Most legal scholars believe that men-only registration would not meet these tests. Thus, in the event of a challenge, the Supreme Court is likely to strike down the 1948 law which gives Carter the authority to register men.

Ultimately, treating men and women equally for purposes of registration is a simple matter of social justice. For years, women have demanded the same educational, job, and financial opportunities as men. Although equality remains a goal rather than reality, women now must be willing to accept what they view as the negative side of the coin. "We will have a terrible backlash if we tell guys on the assembly line to move over when it comes to building Navy ships but scream 'we're different' when we're asked to sail on them," asserts Representative Barbara Mikulski, Democrat of Maryland.

Phyllis Schlafly, national chairman of Stop ERA, had to chortle when leading feminists, overcome by their antiwar pasts, recently played right into her hands. Although their message was against registration altogether, the general public saw "libbers"—including Representative Patricia Schroeder, Democrat of Colorado, former representative Bella Abzug, and journalist Gloria Steinem—who for a decade have demanded equal rights, yell "wait a minute" at the first suggestion that women might be drafted. "They look like a bunch of flakes and hypocrites," complains an activist with impeccable feminist credentials.

As a tactical matter, registering women would probably brighten dimming prospects for ratification of the Equal Rights Amendment. Schlafly would be deprived of her most persuasive and fear-evoking argument against ERA—that it would lead to drafting women. With registration, equal treatment of men and women in the military would be a moot point. Indeed, some feminists contend that registration of women itself could be the biggest step toward equality in the last decade. "It would be a message that Congress is willing to say in a way that nobody can not understand that women are equal," claims Holly Knox, director of the Project on Equal Education Rights.

Despite the clear-cut social and constitutional cases, registration of women faces an uphill but hardly quixotic battle in Congress. As one would expect, there is a sizable block of Schlafly disciples who hold the anachronistic view of women as delicate creatures of limited abilities. Yet they are a minority, as indicated by the 1978 vote extending the ratification period of ERA. But the large influx of younger lawmakers over the last six years has considerably improved the climate on women's issues. In fact, it's tough to find anyone who agrees with House Speaker Tip O'Neill's claim that there is overwhelming opposition to registration of women. "It's not the opposition that is overwhelming," says White House lobbyist William Cable. "It's the desire not to have to face the issue that's overwhelming."

Most legislators are keeping their options open, waiting to see how their constituents line up. But the basis is there for a broad-based coalition led primarily by moderates. In the House, representatives Gladys Spellman, Lindy Boggs, Olympia Snowe, and Barbara Mikulski already have come down firmly in support of registering women as well as men. Kassebaum, a moderate Republican from Kansas, has gone even farther out front in the Senate, at one point publicly challenging O'Neill. These are precisely the women whose support is vital if the issue is to be won. Most of them are not perceived as bra-burners and have substantial credibility with their colleagues. "Gladys and Lindy in particular have big skirts that a few of us have hidden behind on women's issues before," acknowledges a House Democrat.

And politically speaking, the opposition of Abzug and Schroeder could be a plus. Abzug was asked to stay away from the House floor when the ERA extension was up.

Schroeder isn't much more popular. As one House Democrat leader pointed out, "The lights go out when Schroeder goes on."

Still, the political balance of power on this issue lies with the liberals of both parties, particularly those—such as senators Gaylord Nelson, Bob Packwood, and John Danforth—who aren't high on registration but believe that if it's going to happen women should be cut in. The key may be at what point they concede defeat on the first battle and begin the second.

Barring a dramatic turn of events, men are going to be registered. President Carter formally will invoke his authority to do so in mid-June or early July. Although there will be a fight, there is more than a solid majority in both houses to appropriate the additional $20 million or so that Carter needs to revitalize the Selective Service System.

Registration of women must be specifically authorized by Congress, however. The White House will send up separate legislation for this purpose. With the whales on both sides lined up firmly against it, the administration bill will be killed in House and Senate Armed Services Committees. Thus, the showdown will occur on some related defense legislation to which authority to encode women would be offered as an amendment. The most likely vehicle is the annual military authorization bill, which usually comes up for floor action late in the spring.

To have a shot at winning, the pro-ERA network—including groups such as the National Organization for Women, who oppose registration altogether—must pull together to counterbalance Schlafly's efficient and vocal band. It's not that women's groups can deliver that many votes on Capitol Hill. What is crucial is that they organize and generate the grassroots lobbying pressure on congressmen to make them think twice about unequal treatment of men and women. Without such a lobbying effort, which proved extremely successful on the ERA extension, politicians have no incentive to include women nor, more importantly, to have any fear of the consequences if they don't.

"We will work them one-on-one up here, but what people do back home is going to be all important," Gladys Spellman points out. "If they're hearing all negative, they're going to be hard to move."

If the feminists fail to put aside their differences and unite on this issue, they will bear the bulk of responsibility for a defeat which Holly Knox warns would be "terribly damaging to the entire equal rights movement." They will have only themselves to blame for legislating and perpetuating inequality.

## THE DRAFT: WHO NEEDS IT?[3]

First, the good news. All this attention to the possibility of drafting women has killed one major right-wing argument against the Equal Rights Amendment. It will *not* make women vulnerable to the draft. Congress has always had the power to draft women at the whim of its simple majority.

Now, the bad news. We could end up *with* the draft—and *without* the Equal Rights Amendment.

After traveling around this country for a month, talking with women's groups during what accidentally turned out to be the peak of the Great Draft Debate, I can report a spontaneous and populist anger. Not only do women share the general suspicion that this peacetime draft is dangerous and unnecessary, for both women and men, but there is an added frustration with this debate that rarely mentions equal rights in return for equal sacrifice. As one draft-age woman said to Washington TV cameras, "I'm not going anywhere. Not unless it's a national emergency—and I get some equality first."

Some of the more history-minded women have cited the example of suffragists during World War I—who burned President Wilson's speeches in the streets, and generally de-

[3] Reprint of magazine article. *Ms.* 8:20. Ap. '80. Written by Gloria Steinem. Reprinted with permission. Copyright Ms. Foundation for Education & Communication, Inc., 1980.

nied America's right to claim "a war for democracy"—until Wilson put some political force behind the right to vote. They point out that, after a struggle of 70 years, it was probably no accident that the amendment finally passed Congress in 1919 and was ratified less than two years later.

Could our civil disobedience toward a current draft create similar pressure on behalf of the ERA? It's a question often asked on campus, and one that underlines the subversive potential of Women's Studies.

In more private and paranoid moments, feminists wonder aloud if some fraction of the sudden Establishment enthusiasm for a nondiscriminatory draft isn't also a desire, conscious or otherwise, to punish women for demanding a more far-reaching equality. As Florynce Kennedy used to say about an earlier insistence that women "go get killed in Vietnam" to earn equality, "It's as if some men were saying: 'You won't stay weak enough for me to hold the door open for you? Okay, I'll slam it on your hand.'"

The other side of the same coin is a suspicion that many Congressmen are supporting the draft to satisfy their masculinity-proving needs for national primacy or aggression (at the expense of younger men, of course), but still excluding women in order to sugar-coat discrimination, avoid the political wrath of the ultraright-wing, and pass the buck to the courts. (If there's one thing that lawyers agree on, whether they work for the Defense Department or the Coalition Against Registration and the Draft, it's the fact that enough gender-based discrimination has been struck down over the years to build a solid precedent for declaring a male-only draft to be unconstitutional.) Even if women's groups didn't challenge total exclusion, groups representing draft-age men certainly would.

In fact, right-wing opposition to drafting women raises a paranoid suspicion that I thought was mine alone; at least, until I heard so many other women voice the same idea. Why do the same forces that tolerate women's injury and death for lack of Medicaid abortions—as well as condemning battered women's centers and supporting an equal-opportunity death penalty—still "protect" women from the military? "They're just afraid women will learn how to use guns," explained one woman calmly to shouts and applause in a Seattle auditorium.

"It was bad enough when so many black men learned how to fight in Vietnam," said one union woman in Detroit. "But can you imagine what would happen if all the rape victims and battered women and underpaid waitresses and welfare mothers and just plain angry wives got some military training?"

Even discounting this motive of fear, there must be some reluctance to give up war as an all-male game. Otherwise, why are women in most branches still discriminated against in recruitment criteria (in spite of reforms by the Army, higher educational levels and test scores are demanded of most military women) and high technology or sensitive decision-making positions even outside combat? Why is it okay for nurses and communications officers to get shot at and killed in combat zones—but not okay for them to be trained to shoot back?

The National Organization for Women concludes from its research that, if women volunteers were not discriminated against, even in the noncombatant jobs they now want and choose, current military needs could be met *without* a peacetime draft, for men or women. That would mean ending the bias that now causes the army to spend about $3,500 more to recruit a man than a woman—plus creating more accurate definitions of what is and is not a combat job—but the result might save young men from getting drafted at all.

That's not a bad offer. Women can be pardoned for suspicions about why it's refused.

Of course, officer experience in some major command is still normally required for promotions, so lack of combat experience would keep women out of top decision-making posts. Though women are just as fierce as men in self-defense, as Margaret Mead's cross-cultural studies show, we are culturally less likely to engage in or support violence for any reason short of self-defense. (In public opinion polls, American women have been measurably less likely than men to support military solutions, from World War I through Vietnam; as well as more likely to oppose capital punishment, support gun control, and otherwise to be skeptical of violence.) Many military experts point to these cultural facts as reasons why women can't be trusted in combat or decision-making. But women point to these same facts as reasons why we *should* be a part of any military—and in numbers large enough to make our socialized differences felt.

In Illinois, activists are arguing that the ERA would allow some women into previously all-male military preserves, but it would also allow some men into the noncombatant jobs that women have occupied exclusively. "Antidraft, antiwar men should be working to get the ERA passed," said one feminist theorist. "It could create more alternatives for men and have more impact on the military than burning draft cards ever did."

As for what President Carter and Congress should do, the first choice of the majority of women I met in my travels was clear: institute no peacetime draft at all for women or for men, and eliminate discrimination against women inside the military.

The last and worst choice was also clear: a male-only draft that would both perpetuate injustice and heighten the Cold War.

Carter chose the next-to-worst choice: registering both women and men. That makes us equal partners in resisting the draft, should we choose that path; but still unequal partners in the military, should we choose it.

We're heading toward equal sacrifice—but without equal control over when and whether that sacrifice should be made.

## ANNIE, DON'T GET YOUR GUN[4]

One of my favorite possessions, which I picked up a few years ago at a flea market, is a copy of the December 21, 1942, issue of *Life.* At $1.00, it cost me ten times what it would have cost my mother, who graduated from high school

[4] Excerpted from magazine article by Mary Jo Salter, staff editor, *Atlantic.* 245:83–6. Je. '80. Copyright © 1980, by The Atlantic Monthly Company, Boston, Mass. Reprinted with permission.

that year, or my father, who was soon to enlist in the Navy. Recently, as my generation has begun to face the possibility of a peacetime draft registration that would include both sexes, I have found that my issue of *Life*, once no more than a period piece, has gained a timely poignance. In its portrayal of a nation obsessed with war, and with the roles men and women should play in war, it suggests a number of disturbing comparisons with our present situation.

The sacrifices necessary to war pervade not only most of the articles but many of the advertisements in *Life*'s 1942 Christmas issue. "Please don't call long distance *this* Christmas!" Bell Telephone requests. "It may be the 'holiday season'—but war needs the wires. . . ."

*Life*'s vision of a nation united in war—so different from the only American war I remember, Vietnam, during which my older brother's registration as a conscientious objector brought me nothing but relief—is also that of a society comfortably and securely stratified according to what we now popularly call role-models. An ad for the New Haven Railroad shows a soldier in his berth contemplating "a dog named Shucks, or Spot, or Barnacle Bill. The pretty girl who writes so often . . . that gray-haired man, so proud and awkward at the station . . . the mother who knit the socks he'll wear soon. . . ."

Our society's ambivalence about drafting women derives from a certain amount of progress: we no longer hold an (insulting) consensus about what distinguishes women from men. Since President Carter announced his intention to register nineteen- and twenty-year-old women for the draft, however, the debate seems to have taken on an unfortunate rigidity. If you are a "feminist," you may deplore registration and the draft, but you must concede that if men are to be drafted then women should also be drafted. (You are permitted some leeway in determining whether women should actually enter combat.) Only if you are a "non-feminist," however, are you allowed the privilege of questioning the wisdom of doubling the number of potential war-wagers. Yet to frame the debate in such terms is to take an occluded view of what feminism can be.

Most of the debate has focused on three issues: whether women, as people who do not have full rights in this country, should be subject to a draft; the physical differences between men and women and the possible differences in their performance in combat; and last, what weight should be given to traditionally sacrosanct notions of motherhood and femininity. President Carter, who would belong to the "feminist" camp, put his position on the first issue craftily: "Equal responsibilities deserve equal rights." The responsibilities would come first—in life, as in that sentence. And in the April *Atlantic*, James Fallows argued that if women are not drafted, "their claim for equal treatment elsewhere becomes less compelling." Others have spoken of acceding to women's registration as a way to justify and ensure the passage of the ERA. Nevertheless, in recent polls which tell us that more men than women believe that women should be required to engage in combat, one occasionally senses not support for, but a backlash against, the women's movement. Isn't there, perhaps, a certain eagerness to send women off to be killed, as if to say, What do you think of your liberation now? But the objection to "equal responsibilities first" may, in the end, conceal a prescription for anarchy: should minority groups or the poor be subject to a draft before gaining full rights?

The issue of women in combat is made problematic by the increasingly narrow definition of combat and the increasingly technological aspects of war. But the arguments against women in combat are overwhelming: lower endurance, weaker musculature, and, most compellingly, vulnerability to sexual assault. Modern warfare, after all, still requires considerable strength—if not in every situation, in an unpredictable mix of occasions on which women would be at a perilous disadvantage. Women are as likely as men to be taken prisoners of war, and although no form of torture can be dismissed, women would certainly be more vulnerable to one torture—rape—than men. If the likelihood of rape has been belittled by some, even less attention has been paid to the related problems of pregnancy and childbirth in such a situation.

A recent article in *Newsweek* concluded, ambiguously,

that registration could not be considered "egalitarian" unless "women take part in combat. The country could choose to move in that direction, but that would mean overcoming centuries of cultural tradition and accepting the very real physical limitations of women." Our society may have to "accept"—i.e. accommodate itself to—the notion that women should be able to serve as traffic cops, or plumbers, or jockeys; but in the case of international combat, who is being asked to "accept" a woman's physical limitations? A particularly gallant Soviet soldier? Or the woman herself?

The remainder of the debate has focused on the special place of women, particularly as symbols of motherhood, in our society. (One observer found little room for argument. In a recent interview with *U.S. News & World Report*, sociologist and military personnel expert Nora Scott Kinzer revealed that "we are brought up with a myth that women are nicer than men, that they are the keepers of the hearth and the mothers." The myth that women are the mothers will, I suspect, die hard.) President Carter originally called for the registration of those from eighteen to twenty-six, and then narrowed his request to include only nineteen- and twenty-year-olds. Of his several reasons for this, one was that fewer people in the younger age group have family responsibilities. James Fallows, who supports Carter's recommendation, allows that "it is troubling to think of women in combat, or of mothers being drafted, and a sensible draft law would have to recognize such exceptions." It *is* troubling to think of women in combat, or of nursing mothers being drafted; but after the child is no longer physically dependent on the mother, what justification remains for distinguishing between the responsibilities of parents? If the rights and responsibilities of men and women are not only equal but identical, why should women be the baby-sitters first? Well, perhaps there's something to be said for drafting women: it might impress upon us the need for a responsible day-care system.

Such valid feminist questions are not the only issue, however. As journalists inform us repeatedly of how capable our 150,000 women troops are—how skilled, how strong, how necessary to America's preservation—their understandable zeal to applaud the advances women have made in the most male of institutions has at times overshadowed our knowledge of the horrors of war itself. In *The New Republic*, Lisa Myers wrote of women not merely accepting, but *winning*, the right to be drafted. In the same issue, Deborah Shapley unfacetiously suggested that assigning women to combat, as to firefighting and police work at home, would "follow a great American tradition" of "women in all sorts of exciting and dangerous jobs." War isn't hell, sisters—*it's fun.*

Feminists who opposed the draft during Vietnam find themselves accused of cowardice and inconsistency if they oppose a draft now. President Carter has been disturbed (he said) that so many considered a draft inevitable when he proposed registration; but since he coupled this proposal with a military threat to the Soviets, one would have to be extremely short-sighted not to expect both a draft and the serious possibility of war. The suggestion that a military solution to our overdependency on foreign oil would be dangerous to the entire world, and morally shoddy, is one that can respectably be made by both sexes. And it is arguable by both sexes that a peacetime draft, whatever its social justifications, could ironically perpetuate the notion of war's "inevitability." Some "non-feminists" believe that the image of a female soldier being brought home in a body-bag is somehow more hideous than that of a male soldier. But it is hard for anyone to argue that a woman's life is more sacred than a man's, and so if the image seems particularly horrific it serves at least to illustrate how millennia of war have hardened us to the *reality* of young lives lost—lives that happened to be male.

I'll go a step further, admittedly onto boggy ground. The perception of war as natural, even inevitable, is historically a male one. If the world had always been composed solely of women—a prospect as dull as it is impossible—we might not have invented war, or at least not developed it into the world's costliest technological art. We will never know, of course. Women who are currently heads of governments may be as comfortable with the rhetoric of the Cold War as their male counterparts, but such women came to power by adhering to masculine traditions of how power ought to be wielded. That is less an observation about the God-given nature of power than it is about the masculine corner on the market of ideas.

But now women have a little more power as a class. And many of them would tell me that to distinguish between masculine and feminine temperaments is to endanger the progress that women have made. I have no certain evidence—although we may eventually be provided it—that the lesser aggressiveness or physical expression of hostility in women is a biological trait. It is indisputably a socialized trait. But the crucial fact at our disposal is that only a handful of women have fought in combat in all of human history. The explanation for this fact is both that it was a predictable corollary to the discrimination against women in most endeavors, and that war has been specifically a man's game. Only men, after all, can be accused of unmanly behavior if they object to war. It seems to me that in 1980, women interested in effecting a human liberation might have a piece of history in their hands waiting to be molded. What if they gave a registration and none of us came?

I am not the first person to make an argument along these lines: that feminism and pacifism can be profitably linked. The idea is as old as *Lysistrata*. In 1938 Virginia Woolf attempted, in her long essay *Three Guineas*, to answer a question put to her by a man: How are we to prevent war? Interestingly, Woolf's tentative answer involved not the powers that be, but those who traditionally held no power. Because women comprised an unofficial "Society of Outsiders," she felt they owed their government nothing in wartime: "not to fight with arms," "to refuse in the event of war to make munitions or to nurse the wounded," and "not to incite their brothers to fight, but to maintain an attitude of complete indifference." She justified this last, most controversial assertion by claiming that indifference garners more attention than hotblooded partisanship. She also claimed that as a man cannot appreciate a woman's maternal instinct, "it is a fact that she cannot understand what instinct compels him. . . . As fighting thus is a sex characteristic she cannot share, so it is an instinct she cannot judge."

Modern feminists would have trouble accepting that position. Some would answer that parenthood-for-everybody is as trumped-up an "instinct" as courtly love. Others would answer that the paternal instinct, equal to the maternal, has been unrightfully quashed by society. But does it necessarily follow that fighting cannot be a sex characteristic? Nature doesn't keep a scoreboard. The logic that asserts such differences are *impossible* is one with the logic that makes women deny their lesser physical strength. We are not lesser human beings, after all, if we're shorter or don't enjoy playing with tin soldiers. In any case, some of us—myself included—would disagree with Woolf that we have no right to dissuade our brothers from fighting.

What is absolutely timely in *Three Guineas*, however, is Woolf's understanding that women have traditionally abetted war by supporting it once begun. . . . Women have helped perpetuate the male assumption that war is inevitable. How are we to prevent war? In answer, Woolf decided to offer one symbolic guinea to each of three causes: one to provide women with formal education, not just tutoring at home; one to help women enter the professions; and a third guinea "to assert the rights of all . . . to the respect in their persons of the great principles of justice, equality and liberty."

While this may sound like familiar and tattered rhetoric, the conditions Woolf put on the gift of her guineas were far from conventional. She would support *an* education of women, but of a different sort: "not the arts of dominating other people; not the arts of ruling, of killing, of acquiring land and capital." Women needed to enter the male-dominated professions to gain financial self-sufficiency, and the attendant likelihood that they would then be heard. But women outside the professions should still, Woolf felt, be paid for their services. "Is the work of a mother, of a wife, of a daughter, worth nothing to the nation in solid cash?" she demanded.

Finally—and this point is especially compelling—she

cautioned that women must not indiscriminately follow the example of men trapped in professionalism; they must earn sufficient money and properly apply their power, but must not become pugnacious and greedy. For the professions, she wrote, tend to "make the people who practice them possessive, jealous of any infringement of their rights, and highly combative if anyone dares dispute them . . . and do not such qualities lead to war?"

It seems a far-fetched reaction to a call for draft registration, perhaps, for me to reiterate Woolf's question. But I think it is an explosive question for the new generation of women who are both draft-eligible and professionally inclined. To be man's equal, must we share his wardrobe of three-piece suits and military uniforms? It may be understandable, but is certainly regrettable, that "equality" in so many cases means conformity to the male habit. To earn the right to speak our minds, must we agree that we've always been "highly combative," or that we ought to let them teach us how to be? Too often we've been told that to be dedicated professionals, we must eagerly sacrifice all for our jobs and neglect our children (if our offices allow us time to give birth at all). Now, to be dedicated citizens—and feminists—we must accept the male notion of citizenship as including compulsory military service. We are not nearly assertive enough, I think. If we were, we would balk at the all-encompassing view that equality means identicality—and that identicality, to return to the clothing metaphor, means that both sexes wear pants, not skirts.

Women's registration is having a tough time in Congress. That enlisted women soldiers now train for quasi-combat situations, however, and in increasing numbers, may make the objections to women's registration eventually seem academic. On a recent forum on women in war at Harvard Law School, Undersecretary of the Air Force Antonia Chayes, who hopes and expects to see women employed in every aspect of the military, put the point bluntly. In another generation, she said, the objections to women's registration "will all seem rather quaint."

Even if Congress refuses Carter's proposal this time, lawsuits have already been threatened against the government to argue that a solely male draft is unconstitutional. Yet the point is not to protect women, but to devote our energies to preventing any war, particularly between superpowers, in the nuclear age. And women, still the Society of Outsiders, can be specifically instrumental in that prevention. Today I will offer a fourth guinea to the Society to Prevent Woman's Indiscriminate Imitation of Man. For such imitation, which is not synonymous with citizenship, will liberate neither sex from the next "inevitable" war.

---

## DRAFT WOMEN? THE ARGUMENTS FOR AND AGAINST[5]

Reprinted from *U.S. News & World Report*

---

Now awaiting a decision by the Supreme Court is an issue with far-reaching implications for millions of young Americans: Whether the exclusion of women from draft registration unconstitutionally discriminates against men.

The ruling could leave present policies intact. Or it might result either in millions of young women registering—and perhaps some day serving—or in the draft-registration system collapsing altogether.

The case, which passed a milestone on March 24 when the Justices heard oral arguments, was filed by three Philadelphia men in 1971 in protest against U.S. military involvement in Vietnam. The case lay dormant from the time the draft was suspended in 1973 until last year, when President Jimmy Carter ordered a resumption of draft registration as part of the U.S. response to the Soviet Union's invasion of Afghanistan.

Carter asked Congress to finance registration of both sexes, but lawmakers voted to include only men. The anti-draft lawsuit was revived, and last July a panel of three fed-

---

[5] Reprint of staff-written magazine article. *U.S. News & World Report.* 90:30–1. Ap. 6, '81.

eral judges in Philadelphia ruled that males-only registration was unconstitutional. At the government's request, the Supreme Court suspended the ruling pending its own decision in the case, and draft registration for men turning 18 has continued. Although 5.3 million men have registered, no inductions have been ordered.

President Reagan opposed draft registration during his campaign for the White House. But many of his advisers believe it should be retained, and the President has not acted on the issue since assuming office.

The Supreme Court is expected to rule before it adjourns in June. Here are major arguments from briefs submitted to the Justices and the hearing before the Court.

### The Case for Registering Women
As presented by Donald L. Weinberg, attorney for the
Philadelphia men who filed the suit.

*There is no legal justification for males-only registration.*
"All young men, fit or unfit, but no women, however fit to serve, are compelled to register." A program that "places in jeopardy basic personal liberties and ultimately life itself" has no legal basis for excluding one sex.

The Supreme Court previously has struck down "governmental decisions to subject men alone to a burden from which women are automatically exempt" except when such discrimination serves "important governmental objectives." The case in point: The Court's 1976 ruling invalidating an Oklahoma law that allowed women to buy beer at age 18 but barred men from doing so until age 21.

Here, federal authorities have not proved that a men-only registration process is needed to achieve a valid U.S. goal: Raising adequate armed forces.

*Congress abused its authority to set policy for the military by omitting women from draft registration.*
On military issues such as the draft, are not courts bound to accept "a policy decision by Congress, whether wise or unwise?" asked Chief Justice Warren Burger. No, replied

Weinberg. Though courts typically do not interfere with internal military concerns, this issue affects civilians.

Weinberg charged that when Congress wrote the draft law in 1948, it acted "in an atmosphere permeated by male chauvinism." Burger retorted, "Since when is it the function of the courts to inquire into atmospheres?"

Associate Justice Potter Stewart said that the Philadelphia men were "putting the cart before the horse" by demanding that Congress justify its decision to exclude women. "An act of Congress is presumed valid, and it's up to you to prove that it is not," he told Weinberg.

Judges are empowered to strike down military policies that are biased against women, Weinberg argued. In 1973, the Supreme Court declared unconstitutional laws that gave military men housing and health allowances for their spouses but limited such aid for spouses of military women.

*Many women already serve as volunteers.*

"Both the military and Congress have made concerted efforts over the last decade to increase the role of women in the armed forces."

Now, 8.4 percent of the nation's 2 million armed services personnel are female, and the proportion is going up. It is irrational to continue to exclude women from draft registration if U.S. policy is to give them expanded military duties.

Weinberg told the Justices that keeping women out of draft eligibility would be "excluding from the pool to whom we can turn in an emergency ... the very skills we have sought to bring into the armed forces."

*Even though federal rules bar women from combat, most military jobs are classified as noncombat.*

Subjecting women to the draft would increase military flexibility. In an emergency, women would be among those best qualified for noncombat jobs, "and their availability would free more combat-trained soldiers for quicker redeployment to battle."

Women draftees would be qualified for tens of thousands of military jobs. In fact, a Defense Department official told Congress last year that if a mobilization were necessary, military leaders would like 80,000 out of a total of 650,000 inducted to be women.

*Excluding women from registration "perpetuates . . . ancient sexual stereotypes."*

The courts have held that laws based on outmoded views of the roles of men and women must be condemned—in part because they may be "self-fulfilling prophecies." In this case, the old "idea that men are meant for war and women solely for the home and hearth" should be discarded.

Added representatives of 11 women's-rights groups who filed a brief supporting the challenge to men-only registration: "The exclusion of women . . . is based solely on archaic notions of women's proper place in society that in the past prompted 'protective' labor laws and the exclusion of women from juries and the legal profession. Until women assume their equal share of societal obligations, they will retain their inferior status."

### *The Case Against Women's Registration*
As presented by Wade H. McCree, Jr., solicitor general of the U.S.

*Congress traditionally has decided U.S. military policy.*
Excluding women from registration must be upheld because of "the power expressly granted to Congress by the Constitution . . . to raise an army." Because of that provision, this case differs from other kinds of sex-bias suits. Here, it is inappropriate for a court "to substitute its judgment for that of Congress. . . . Congress knew exactly what it was doing when it refused to require the registration of women."

Five congressmen who filed a brief warned that if women are forced to register, courts would be asked to decide related questions such as whether men and women must be drafted in equal numbers.

*Since women are ineligible for combat assignments, they need not be required to register for the draft.*

History shows that most draftees are sent into combat. In addition, "in recent years, more than sufficient numbers of women have been volunteering to staff those noncombat positions for which they are eligible." Even in the event of a mobilization, enough women would sign up to avoid the need for a draft.

Forcing women to register would cost taxpayers about 8.5 million dollars but would accomplish nothing.

The Senate Armed Services Committee concluded that "processing and training would be needlessly burdened by women recruits who could not be used in combat."

Furthermore, an influx of women would lessen military flexibility. When combat troops are to be rotated into noncombat jobs after assignments in the field, many of those positions would already have been filled by women. "The nation's ability to respond with maximum speed and efficiency would be compromised." What the military needs most are persons of "maximum flexibility," such as male nurses who can be shifted to combat if necessary.

It is possible that the armed forces at some point will decide that women should be allowed to fill combat positions. If that happens, the draft-registration law can be amended.

*Sex discrimination in the armed forces can be constitutional, even though other forms of bias are not.*

Associate Justice William Brennan asked McCree, "Could Congress decide to register only Negroes?" McCree replied, "That would not be legitimate." Brennan then asked, "Could Congress include or exclude people based on religion?" McCree said, "That would not be legitimate, either." Brennan concluded the exchange by remarking that in McCree's view, "gender" seemed to be the only appropriate form of bias in the military.

A 1975 Supreme Court case was cited by McCree as an example of valid sex bias. In that ruling, the Justices upheld a law that provided that male naval officers be discharged after twice failing to be promoted within 10 years but allowed female officers a 13-year period before being forced out. The Court said Congress had the power to enact different standards for male and female military officers if there was a rational reason for doing so.

*Forcing women into the military would harm society.*

In a brief filed in support of the Justice Department's position, 16 women argued that Congress properly found that the drafting of women "would place unprecedented strains on family life." Noting that only women can bear children, they argue that "even slight uncertainty as to when and how she will be required to fulfill a draft obligation can seriously affect a woman's plans."

The women contend also that "the potential absence of a mother from a home is . . . more likely to be disruptive than the potential absence of a father." Many women fear sexual abuse and invasions of personal privacy if they are forced into the military, and they generally regard military service "as repugnant and inappropriate to the female gender," the women asserted.

# BIBLIOGRAPHY

An asterisk (*) preceding a reference indicates that the article or part of it has been reprinted in this book.

## BOOKS AND PAMPHLETS

Barnet, R. J. Real security: restoring American power in a dangerous decade. Simon & Schuster. '81.

Binkin, Martin and Kyriakopolous, Irene. Youth or experience? Manning the modern military. Brookings Institution. '79.

Bliven, Bruce Jr. Volunteers one and all. Reader's Digest Press. '76.

Fallows, James. National defense. Random House. '81.

Gabriel, R. A. and Savage, P. L. Crisis in command: mismanagement in the army. Hill & Wang. '78.

Janowitz, Morris. The professional soldier: a social and political portrait. Free Press. '71.

*Kojm, C. A. The ABC's of defense. (Headline series) Foreign Policy Association, Inc. 205 Lexington Ave. New York, NY 10016. '81.

Marmion, H. A. The case against a volunteer army. Quadrangle. '71.

## PERIODICALS

America. 142:93–4. F. 9, '80. Marching toward the draft, maybe.

*America. 142:95–7. F. 9, '80. About-face on the draft. R. A. Gabriel.

America. 142:237–8. Mr. 22, '80. Proposal did not register.

America. 142:532–3. Je. 28, '80. Draft registration: crying wolf.

*America. 143:46–9. Ag. 2–9, '80. The draft: an occasion of sin? G. C. Zahn.

*America. 144:139–40. F. 21, '81. President Reagan and registration for the draft. J. A. Tetlow.

*Atlantic. 245:34–8+. Ap. '80. Why the Army needs it. J. R. Webb.

*Atlantic. 245:44–7. Ap. '80. Why the country needs it. J. M. Fallows.

*Atlantic. 245:83–6. Je. '80. Annie, don't get your gun. M. J. Salter.

Christian Century. 96:430–1. Ap. 18, '79. Draft: is it coming back?
    Thomas Conrad.
Christian Century. 97:62–3. Ja. 23, '80. Draft is coming. C. E.
    Fager.
Christianity & Crisis. 39:306+. D. 10, '79. Stopping the draft in
    Congress. Murray Polner.
Christianity Today. 24:74+. S. 5, '80. Churches go on offensive
    over draft registration.
Commonweal. 106:425–6. Ag. 3, '79. Draft no, assassins yes. John
    Garvey.
°Commonweal. 106:553–5. O. 12, '79. Against the draft: opening
    Pandora's box. Murray Polner.
°Commonweal. 106:555–7. O. 12, '79. Against the all-volunteer
    force. H. A. Marmion.
Commonweal. 107:487–8. S. 12, '80. Saving the generals. Frank
    Getlein.
Congressional Quarterly Weekly Report. 37:735+. Ap. 21, '79.
    The draft issue: resumption of registration of 18-year-olds
    considered. Pat Towell.
°Economist. 279:23–5. Ap. 25, '81. Today's American army.
Esquire. 93:11–13. My. '80. Suppose there was a war ... Richard
    Reeves.
°Fortune. 101:52–4+. Ap. 7, '80. It's time to bite the bullet on the
    draft. Juan Cameron.
°Fortune. 102:169–70. Jl. 14, '80. Draft is an unfair tax on unlucky
    young men [interview by A. Morrison]. W. H. Meckling.
Harpers. 259:16+. D. '79. Too few good men. Seth Cropsey.
°Ms. 8:20+. Ap. '80. Draft: who needs it? Gloria Steinem.
°Nation. 229:353+. O. 20, '79. Drive to revive the draft. B. M.
    Gross.
Nation. 230:132. F. 9, '80. Draft dodge.
Nation. 230:359–62. Mr. 29, '80. Citizen's guide to draft deter-
    rence. B. M. Gross.
Nation. 231:141. Ag. 16–23, '80. Famous victory. B. M. Gross.
National NOW Times. p 1. My. '80. NOW brief filed in landmark
    draft registration case.
National Review. 32:847. Jl. 11, '80. Reflections on the draft. Mi-
    chael Novak.
°New Republic. 182:15–19. Mr. 1, '80. Giant step toward equal-
    ity? Lisa Myers.
New Republic. 183:20–3. Jl. 5–12, '80. Son of Sad Sack. W. P.
    Snyder.
Newsweek. 95:29. F. 4, '80. Is the draft really needed? M. Beck
    and others.

*Newsweek. 95:79. F. 11, '80. Draft registration. M. Friedman.

*Newsweek. 95:34–6+. F. 18, '80. Women in the armed forces. M. Beck and others.

Newsweek. 95:120. F. 18, '80. Armies should win wars. G. F. Will.

Newsweek. 95:17. Mr. 10, '80. Antidraft youths think of Canada. Eileen Keerdoja and Anthony Collings.

Newsweek. 95:40+. Mr. 10, '80. Carter's draft plan loses a skirmish. A. J. Mayer and D. C. Martin.

Newsweek. 95:27. Je. 23, '80. Uncle Sam wants you to register.

Newsweek. 96:36. Jl. 28, '80. Draft sign-up: off again, on again.

Newsweek. 96:24. Ag. 4, '80. Signing up—and sitting in. M. Beck and others.

New York. 12:39–42. Ap. 2, '79. Back to basic at Fort Dix. Ralph Schoenstein.

*New York Times Magazine. p. 12. Jl. 27, '80. Draft. R. Baker.

Progressive. 43:32–6. Je. '79. Reviving the draft. R. A. Seeley.

Progressive. 43:50–1. D. '79. Best-laid plans. Thomas Conrad.

Progressive. 44:66. Ja. '80. Middle-aged soldiers never die . . . J. A. Stegenga.

Progressive. 44:11. Ap. '80. Forced draftin'. R. K. Musil.

*Progressive. 44:23–4. My. '80. Behind the push to revive the draft. Joseph Kelley.

Progressive. 44:47. Je. '80. Pen versus the sword. Thomas Conrad.

Progressive. 44:7. Ag. '80. Time to say no.

Progressive. 44:11. S. '80. It's the law.

*Progressive. 44:38. O. '80. Why I registered for the draft. Christopher Garlock.

*Progressive. 44:39. O. '80. Why I refused to register. Matthew Bunn.

*Saturday Review. 6:8. S. 15, '79. Games nations play; military draft. N. Cousins.

*Society. 17:70–2. N. '79. National service and the all-volunteer force. C. C. Moskos Jr.

Time. 113:18. Ap. 2, '79. Uncle Sam wants who? reinstating the draft.

Time. 115:16. F. 4, '80. Sign-up, but no call-up.

Time. 115:32. F. 11, '80. Reopening an old debate [registration of women].

Time. 115:24. F. 18, '80. Soon, G.I. Jill?

Time. 115:18. F. 25, '80. Greetings . . .

Time. 115:24–7+. Je. 9, '80. Who'll fight for America?

Time. 115:30. Je. 9, '80. Out of step with the rest.

Shelf

Time. 115:86–7. Je. 9, '80.                 ance
Morrow.

Time. 115:9. Je. 23, '80. Male call at the post office: draft registration bill survives a Senate filibuster.

Time. 116:36. Jl. 28, '80. No draft without women too: but a Supreme Court Justice says registration can go on.

Time. 116:20. S. 15, '80. Draft sign-up.

U.S. Catholic. 45:12–17. My. '80. Draft is immoral [with readers' comments]. M. O. Hatfield.

U.S. News & World Report. 86:12. F. 12, '79. Let's see your draft card, lady.

U.S. News & World Report. 86:54–6. Mr. 5, '79. Volunteer Army runs into trouble; with pro and con interviews with J. C. Stennis and Les Aspin.

U.S. News & World Report. 86:76. Ap. 2, '79. Debate over the draft. Marvin Stone.

U.S. News & World Report. 86:62. Je. 11, '79. Behind drive to bring back the draft.

U.S. News & World Report. 88:9. F. 4, '80. If draft resumes—what to expect.

°U.S. News & World Report. 88:37–8. F. 11, '80. Should U.S. revive the draft? [interviews] S. A. Nunn Jr.; M. O. Hatfield.

U.S. News & World Report. 88:84. F. 11, '80. On with draft registration. Marvin Stone.

U.S. News & World Report. 88:7. F. 18, '80. Registration plan cheered, booed.

U.S. News & World Report. 88:28–9. F. 25, '80. In U.S. colleges: the draft again is topic A.

U.S. News & World Report. 88:34. Mr. 10, '80. U.S. almost alone in spurning draft.

°U.S. News & World Report. 88:36. My. 12, '80. Why U.S. must return to the draft [interview]. W. C. Westmoreland.

°U.S. News & World Report. 88:45. Je. 23, '80. How new draft registration rules work.

U.S. News & World Report. 89:7. Jl. 28, '80. New roadblocks to draft registration [Federal-court ruling that plan unconstitutionally discriminated against men].

U.S. News & World Report. 89:24–5. Ag. 4, '80. What's really at stake in draft controversy. R. S. Dudney.

U.S. News & World Report. 89:8. S. 8, '80. New crop of draft evaders?

°U.S. News & World Report. 90:30–1. Ap. 6, '81. Draft women? the arguments for and against.